T0312592

HOW TO

DRINK

LIKE A

SPY

HOW TO DRINK LIKE A
SPY

ALBERT W. A. SCHMID

Foreword by Jon Wiant

RED ⚡ LIGHTNING BOOKS

This book is a publication of

Red Lightning Books
1320 East 10th Street
Bloomington, Indiana 47405 USA

redlightningbooks.com

Manufactured in the United States of America

ISBN 978-1-68435-090-2 (hardback)
ISBN 978-1-68435-091-9 (ebook)

1 2 3 4 5   24 23 22 21 20 19

THIS BOOK IS DEDICATED TO
my godmother,

WENDY FREDLAND

CONTENTS

ONE

The Spy Who Came in for a Drink

TWO

Cocktail Recipes

FOREWORD

I SPENT MOST OF MY adult life as an intelligence officer. In the early years, I spent time in Southeast Asia and Central America. Later, fortune favored me with headquarters assignments. For nearly twenty-five of those years, I was a senior intelligence officer. Southeast Asia and Central America gave way to the halls of Washington, DC, varied bureaucracies replacing the field cultures in which I previously operated. This brief gazette of my career is offered merely to define my operational geography of alcohol, drinks, and cocktails. It also explains how I ended up writing the foreword to this exquisite book by Albert Schmid, chef extraordinaire, professor, writer, master of libations, and dear friend for many years. He thought an old spy was just right to introduce *How to Drink Like a Spy*. I hesitate to add, however, that our paths have never crossed professionally.

This book is essential reading for my profession. Find it in my library next to William Johnson's *Thwarting Enemies at Home and Abroad: How to Be a Counterintelligence Officer*. This remains the best book on spy tradecraft—what you need to know if you are going to make it as a spy. It will be on the shelf with *Spycraft: The Secret History of the CIA's Spytechs, from Communism to Al-Qaeda*, by Robert Wallace and H. Keith Melton, two gentlemen who know spy gadgets better than James Bond's Q. Quite coincidentally, but maybe not so coincidentally, James Olson's *Fair Play: The Moral Dilemmas of Spying* is nearby. Schmid has imaginatively used Jim Olson's Ten Commandments of Counterintelligence as a set of admonitions that link spycraft with mixology. Understand, if not master, these works, and you have a good chance of making it as a spy on the streets. Quite beyond Schmid's practical command of the spy business, his naming of cocktails is brilliant. It is a tribute to those people who populate our spy fiction and, on occasion, inform our spy reality.

What is it about spies and alcohol? It seems to be both the lubricant of our profession and a source for ruination of intelligence officers. Let us get the ruination out of the way. Yes, both real intelligence officers and fictional spies can have a problem with the bottle. The stress of operations, fear of compromise, pressure to recruit, odd hours, wicked travel, lives of deception, whatever, these things can take their toll.

Now, most of us do drink; occasionally, we may even be a bit squiffy or find ourselves three sheets to the wind and come to work the next day with a crushing hangover. Life in the world of foreign affairs can be lubricated, but most of us understand how to enjoy this aspect in moderation. Immoderation is the problem. Some spies give their lives over to alcohol and become alcoholics. The Cambridge Five, the great British spies of the twentieth century, were awash in alcohol. Counterintelligence agents still tell their stories as warnings about the danger of immoderation as a sign of serious security vulnerability. Closer to home, CIA officer Aldrich Ames, one of the most damaging Soviet spies in US history, should have been a poster boy for the security services. He was a binge drinker even before he joined the agency. By mid-career, he was often drunk by noon. He was not alone. As his investigation also revealed, his Russian case officer was also sauced by midday. Confusion reigned when both met clandestinely; nobody could decipher the notes of their drunken ramblings. John le Carré's dissolute British intelligence office Alec Leamas, the antihero of *The Spy Who Came in from the Cold*, was deeply into the bottle. Leamas's drunkenness (or contrived binges) are the occasion for the East German espionage service to recruit the recently fired, perennially drunk ex–case officer.

We could go on in this vein. I am certain that every spy service human resource chief could nominate boozers for our examination. That's not our purpose here other than to make one important observation: boozers suck their alcohol from a bottle, often a bottle in a bag or kept in a desk drawer. They drink to get drunk. They do not just sip cocktails.

Cocktails, on the other hand, are the real lubricants of our profession. Whether enjoyed before a quiet dinner or consumed at a large diplomatic reception or embassy party, they are integral to the whole business of spying. These are the venues where we meet people, cadge introductions, and lay the groundwork for future meetings. Sharing a drink may be the first step in the preparation for eventual seduction or making the first link on a daisy chain of connections. A cocktail invites conversation, and conversation leads to the potential sources who can answer our secret questions. Without this flow of information, we spies have no business. In our training, we learn how to work a reception, practicing elicitation or spotting and assessing. Managing the drink is part of the business, as related by retired MI6 officer Richard Dunn:

> One exercise was meeting a former, high-ranking KGB officer. The brief was really straightforward—he's requested a meeting and you've got to go and find out why he wants to see you. Word of warning: He has already polished off a lot of vodka and you have to match him on that, otherwise there will be a credibility issue. Also, you can't take notes during that meeting because he's really twitchy about that, so you have to memorize, with pinpoint accuracy, anything he says, while at the same time match him on a drinking level.[1]

"Conversation ensued; drinks were shared."[2] Send the first tour officers out to an embassy reception, and count the business cards they've collected. It's the first step in the dance. In this post–Cold War world of terrorist threats and nuclear weapons proliferations, some question whether old-fashioned embassy parties are still relevant. In this new world of spying, corporate receptions, academic conferences, science and technology fairs, and the like are just as productive venues for finding potential assets, and receptions with cocktails are just as common. As the music changes, so must the dance . . . but not that much.

It is James Bond who really puts the professional stamp on the cocktail. The whole world knows how Bond has his martini—"shaken, not stirred," a mantra recognized in drinking establishments around the globe. The Bond martini may be the defining attribute for his world of espionage.

He orders it first in *Casino Royale*. Spy historian Ben Macintyre notes that Bond's drink "was a weaponized martini": "Three measures of Gordons, one of vodka, half a measure of Kina Lillet. Shake it very well until it's ice cold, then add a large thick slice of lemon-peel."[3]

Bond may be best associated with the martini, but later in his career, you suspect that he had a gander or two at Professor Schmid's recipes. Macintyre reports that in *On Her Majesty's Secret Service*, Bond downs no fewer than forty-seven drinks over the course of the book! As you might expect, Bond drinks a lot of wine, very good wine, but the breadth of spirits he consumes is almost encyclopedic:

> Calvados, three bourbon with water, four vodka and tonics, two
> double brandy and ginger ales, two whiskey and soda, three
> double vodka martinis, two double bourbon on the rocks, at
> least one glass of neat whiskey, a flask of Enzian schnapps,
> Marsala wine, the better part of a bottle of fiery Algerian
> wine (served by M), two more scotch whiskeys, half a pint of
> I. W. Harper bourbon, a Jack Daniels's Tennessee whisky with

water, on the rocks, a bottle of Riquewihr wine, four steins of Franziskaner beer, and a double Steinhager gin.[4]

That struck me as a bit excessive, but maybe not that much out of character for a spy. In Washington, I set my own best record for working the circuit by attending an embassy reception or diplomatic dinner party twelve nights in a row! I probably had at least two drinks at each event, perhaps three—or maybe four. I started with a cocktail—my preference was a gin and tonic—and then I switched to wine with dinner or buffet. I had no more than two glasses of wine. Since I was working the crowd, I'd stay for brandy or cordials after the meal. Four drinks, twelve events in two weeks, and I had consumed maybe forty-eight drinks. That maybe put me on the Bond standard.

Dinners are better than receptions because you are more apt to be offered a well-prepared cocktail. It was at a tête-à-tête at the head of station's residence where I had my first Pimm's Cup, a No. 6. The Brits do have their standards. I stayed with gin and tonic as my generic cocktail, but at ritzier receptions I might slip into using brand names: "Oh, I'll have a gin and tonic. Yes, Bruichladdich with Lamb and Watt Hibiscus tonic. No? Sorry. Well then, how about a Bombay Sapphire with Fever Tree?" That is standing up to the game. On occasion where the clearest head was required, I've ordered an Alec Quin: "Oh, a Quin. It's Perrier with just a splash of club soda and the quarter peel of an orange." Good for bringing out puzzlement. It should have a place in the recipes. "Alec Quin" was a name I used once a long time ago—a cover name for a sham cocktail. Perfect.

Once while I was working in Southeast Asia, the British high commissioner in Kuala Lumpur invited me for lunch at his club. I arrived in typical American tropical dress: dark slacks and a white button-down collared shirt with a conservative tie. He greeted me with a bit of a tsk-tsk: "Jon, being in the tropics does not excuse one from being a gentleman." I joined him with a borrowed jacket, and he ordered me a Singapore Sling. All so very, very civilized. The scene would not work with a bottle of beer. Here, a word to the wise: diplomats may order a beer at a reception, but never, ever should one drink from the bottle. Folk under diplomatic cover sometimes forget this sacred rule and try to chat away with a bottle of beer in hand—thereby blowing their cover.

Standards will, however, vary across cultures. In my early days in Vietnam, fifty years ago, some Vietnamese were just experimenting with cocktails. Perhaps experimenting is not the right word; think of it as protomixology. The novelty of mixed drinks was made more speculative by the fact that your host considered anything in a bottle to be "whiskey," and anything in a can was a "mixer." I met my province chief for drinks. I brought him a bottle of Johnnie Walker Red Label as a gift. He insisted we open the bottle then and there. And then I watched in complete disbelief as he poured a double shot of Red Label into a glass and then opened a can of "mixer." He offered me a cocktail made of Johnny Walker Red Label and . . . grape soda! No ice needed. I was seated at a table, and there was a platter in front of me, facing me, with a roasted pig who had Christmas lights in its eye sockets. I've suggested that the professor include that recipe in the second edition of *How to Drink Like a Spy*. It strikes me as fusion cuisine. Call it "No Concord."

A few years later, I was with a gathering of DPs in Frankfurt, Germany. These were displaced persons, refugees from the East, and even in the 1970s there were still a few DP camps left. Each had a kind of rudimentary bar cobbled together of mismatched tables, chairs, and so forth. Our mentors explained that such camps were bargain basements for recruiting spies to work behind the Iron Curtain. It was in one of these bars that I was introduced to a drink that was simply the most abominable concoction I have ever consumed. It beggared the imagination; after a couple of sips, I no longer had the capacity for speech or description. It was made of equal measures of Steinhäger, Jägermeister, and a Bolls liquor; the drink had the consistency of eggnog and the flavor of rotten bananas. I cannot recall whether we actually did any spying business. A drink like that can define your destiny.

This recipe is not found in *How to Drink Like a Spy*, and that is a very good thing. For a potable variation, I suggest Albert Schmid's Spymaster.

Jon Wiant

NOTES

1. Milena Veselinovic, "This Is How You Become a Professional Spy," CNN, November 25, 2015, https://www.cnn.com/2015/11/20/business/james-bond-this-is-how-you-become-a-spy/index.html.

2. Hal Humphreys, "5 Networking Secrets from a Professional Spy," *Fast Company*, October 6, 2014, https://www.fastcompany.com/3036637/5-networking-secrets-from-a-professional-spy.

3. Ben Macintyre, *For Your Eyes Only: Ian Fleming + James Bond* (New York: Bloomsbury Press, 2008), 18–19.

4. Macintyre, 178.

ACKNOWLEDGMENTS

THANKS TO THE FOLLOWING:

My wife, Kim, for her love, support, and copyediting.

My sons, Tom and Mike, for inspiring me always to do my best.

My mother, Elizabeth Schmid, for all of her support and advice.

My father-in-law, Richard E. Dunn, for his mentorship and our wonderful conversations.

My sisters and brothers, Gretchen, Tiffany, Rachel, Justin, Bennett, Ana, Shane, and John, for their support.

My colleagues, the instructors and professors in the Culinary Arts and Hospitality Management Departments at Guilford Technical Community College, including Linda Beitz, Michele Prairie, Al Romano, L. J. Rush, Tom Lantz, and Keith Gardner. Samphanh Soxayachanh, I enjoy starting my business day with your smile and happy nature.

My friend and former student Loreal "the Butcher Babe" Gavin, whose enthusiasm is infectious.

My friend Scot Duval, for his friendly counsel.

My friends Brian and Angie Clute—looking forward to the next trip!

My longtime friend Keith Mellage.

My colleague and friend Deb Walsh, Esq., for her energy, enthusiasm, and smile.

My colleague and fellow PK Dr. Randy Parker, for leading the institution where I teach and the good words each time I see him.

The artists who made me laugh, smile, and dance while working on this project: Justin Timberlake, Jimmy Fallon, James Corden, Ellen DeGeneres, Etta James, Frank Sinatra, Alicia Keys, Jay-Z, Dr. Dre, Bruno Mars, Maroon 5, Michael Bublé, and Snoop Dogg.

SECRET AGENT LEXICON

THE FOLLOWING ARE TERMS RELATED to the intelligence world. These terms come from a wide variety of spy-themed books and movies. All of them have been verified by the text *Terms & Definitions of Interest for Counterintelligence Professionals*, edited by Col. Mark Reagan (Ret.).

Abort To discontinue a mission for any number of reasons.

Access The level to which someone has the ability to obtain classified information.

Advanced persistent threat (APT) Two or more capable adversaries working together.

Agency An organization collecting and/or processing intelligence information.

Agent A person obtaining information (intelligence) for a government agency. An agent reports to a case officer.

Alias A false or alternate identity used for cover during a mission.

Alliance A formal relationship of two or more agencies or countries to support common interests between members.

Ambassador A diplomatic official of the highest order, usually from one country to another. Also known as chief of mission (CoM).

Analysis The process of evaluating intelligence information.

Anomaly Activities outside the norm or expected results.

Apprehension Taking a person into custody.

Assassination A political murder by a sudden or secret attack.

Assessment The judgment of a person or program to judge the accomplishment of goals.

Asset Any resource, human or technical, available to an intelligence service for gathering information.

Asylum Protection granted to a foreign national by the government to prevent persecution of the foreign national by his or her home government.

Authenticate (authentication) A challenge to information, usually by voice or electronic means, to validate the original message or information.

Backdoor A loophole in software used to circumvent security controls.

Backstop (backstopping) Arrangements made to support undercover operatives so that questions asked about the operatives will support the cover story.

Beacon A tracking device that is fastened to a person or object to track the location of that person or object.

Bigot (case or list) A strict need-to-know basis on a case or list of people who are on the need-to-know list related to a case.

Black Clandestine or covert.

Black list People who have been determined to be a threat to friendly forces.

Blow (blown) To reveal person(s) or location(s) related to a covert operation, usually unintentionally, but can also be intentional. In either case, the agent is exposed.

Bug (bugging or bugged) A concealed listening device.

Burn notice An official statement by an agency that an agent, individual, or group is unreliable.

Burned When a case officer or agent is compromised.

Capability The ability to perform a course of action.

Car toss A dead drop where an object is thrown from a car to a preselected site.

Case An intelligence operation.

Case officer Staff officer of an intelligence agency.

Casing Reconnaissance of an area related to a subject.

Cell A small group of people who work together of a specific purpose.

Central Intelligence Agency (CIA) Intelligence agency in the United States tasked with providing intelligence to senior policy makers.

Chain of custody (chain of evidence) A written record of the movement of evidence from the collection, processing, and storage.

Chief of station (CoS) The senior intelligence officer in a foreign country.

Chokepoint A bridge, tunnel, or other area used to channel the movement of an opposing force.

Cipher A code that relies on a cryptographic system of letters, numbers, or symbols that can be decoded based on a set of rules.

Clandestine A secret operation.

Clean Free of surveillance or weapons.

Clearance The level of an individual's formal security access. Three levels of clearance exist in the United States from lowest to highest, confidential, secret, and top secret.

Cobbler A person who specialized in forging passports and other documents.

Code A system of communication between groups.

Codebook A book containing text equivalents of the code for easy decryption.

Code word A classified word or name assigned to an operation or person to safeguard the operation or person.

Collection Gathering intelligence information.

Compromise (compromised) The disclosure of classified information to an unauthorized person.

Concealment The act of remaining hidden.

Contamination The disclosure of information or data from one security level to another security level, usually referring to information moving from a higher level of security to a lower level of security.

Counterintelligence (counterespionage) The activity of detecting and/or neutralizing espionage activities of other countries.

Countermeasures An effort to negate an adversary's efforts to exploit weaknesses or vulnerabilities.

Counterproliferation Actions taken to negate the threat or use of weapons of mass destruction.

Countersurveillance Actions taken to negate hostile surveillance.

Courier A person who, knowingly or unknowingly, moves information or intelligence from one place or person to another.

Cover (covert) Concealment of the identity of a person or mission to safeguard the person or mission.

Covert operation Actions, events, or missions of which a government will deny knowledge or responsibility.

Cultivation The deliberate association with a person with the intent of recruitment or obtaining information.

Cut-out A mutually trusted intermediary who facilitates the transfer of intelligence between two agents.

Debriefing An interview with a willing party to collect information related to a mission.

Decoy A bluff or imitation of a person or object with the intent of deceiving the enemy.

Deep cover A cover that withstands investigation by the opposition.

Defection (defector) A person with intelligence who leaves one country for another (usually enemy) country.

Dossier A file with information on a person.

Double agent An agent who is in contact with two opposing intelligence services but only really works for one.

Dry clean (dry cleaning) An attempt to avoid or lose enemy surveillance.

Encryption The process of securing a message by using a cipher.

Eyewash False entries into a file to protect the source.

False flag An event that is attributed to one country when in reality the event belongs to another; in recruiting an agent who falsely claims to be from one country but actually represents another.

Federal Bureau of Investigation (FBI) The FBI is the domestic security and intelligence agency for the United States. The FBI is the United States' version of MI5 in Great Britain.

Front A legitimate operation or company created by an intelligence agency to provide cover for its agents and operatives.

Ghost surveillance Omnipresent surveillance out of the view of the target.

Handler A case officer or intelligence officer who works with and is directly responsible for the activities of an agent.

Hello number A cut-out telephone where the caller transfers only a codeword to their handler.

Honey trap (honeypot) The use of sexual situations that leave the target vulnerable to blackmail.

Human intelligence (HUMINT) At the heart of the spy business, human intelligence is the collection of intelligence through human sources.

Infiltrate (infiltration) Entering a country or agency by a foreign agent.

Informant A person who provides intelligence to an agent.

Insider threat A person with security clearance who may harm national security by sharing the information.

INTERPOL The world's largest police agency, working across INTERPOL's 188-member state borders.

Interrogation The interview of an unwilling source.

Jack-in-the-box A mannequin placed in a car to deceive surveillance.

Judgment An analytical leap used to fill in gaps in intelligence.

Lead An identified source of intelligence.

Leak Unauthorized disclosure of intelligence.

Meet (alternative meet) A designated place to gather (a secondary location to gather).

MI5 British Security Service that is the British equivalent to the Federal Bureau of Investigation (FBI) in the United States. MI5 is tasked with threats of national security.

MI6 British Secret Intelligence Service that is the British equivalent to the CIA in the United States. MI6 is tasked with foreign intelligence.

Mole An agent who is spying on his or her own organization, usually for another agency.

Need to know A criterion used to determine access to very sensitive information or data; even people with security clearance may have limited or no access unless they have an operational reason for the information.

Office of Strategic Services (OSS) The US World War II predecessor of the CIA.

Overt Activities conducted in the open that are designed to acquire information through legal means without concealment.

Pitch The capital expended to recruit a source.

Rabbit The target of a surveillance operation.

Ravens (Romeo spies) Agents who seduce women who have access to classified information in the hopes the agent can access the intelligence; a male version of a swallow.

Safe house A house or apartment used to afford safety and security for an agent or operation.

Sanitation (sanitize) Editing intelligence as to allow wider distribution.

Sleeper An agent who is assigned to a target area but does not engage in intelligence gathering until ordered to do so if a specific need should arise.

Special Operations Executive (SOE) A British group formed during World War II, known informally as the Baker Street Irregulars, Churchill's Secret Army, and the Ministry of Ungentlemanly Warfare; this agency was responsible for establishing guerrilla organizations in continental Europe.

Spotter An agent assigned to locate people who might be of value to the agency.

Spy A professional intelligence officer.

Surveillance The systematic observation of a target.

Suspect A person who is believed to have committed a crime because of reasonable information or evidence.

Swallow A female agent who uses sex as a tool; the female version of a raven (Romeo) spy.

Sweep To examine a room for surveillance devices.

Target (targeting) A person, agency, or country against which intelligence gathering is directed.

Tracking Following a target to have exact knowledge of the target's location.

Trade craft Methods and equipment used by agents to perform their jobs.

Triple agent Similar to a double agent, but the triple agent works as an agent for three agencies while really working for only one of them.

HOW TO

DRINK

LIKE A

SPY

ONE

The Spy Who Came in for a Drink

DO YOU HAVE WHAT IT takes to be a spy?

Most of us don't have to worry about dying during a normal workday, and those who do usually don't have to worry about someone hunting them down. Torture is not a usual workplace hazard. Our friends know where we work; they know what we do for a living. We don't have to have a cover for our daily lives. After a stressful day of office work, most people look forward to relaxing with friends and family, enjoying a drink while the day's stress fades into the past. Spies don't get that luxury. Many times, not only are they away from family, but they are also isolated, surviving only on their intellect, wits, and tradecraft. The art and science of spying is complex and detailed. A day's work for the spy includes gathering classified information from a foreign country so that he or she can deliver the secret information to his or her home country. And the whole time, agents from the foreign country are working to prevent the spy from returning home. The spy's punishment could be death or, if caught alive, torture (perhaps daily), a long imprisonment, and after a trial, death by hanging or firing squad. Who can forget Nathan Hale's last words when he was caught spying on the British during the Revolutionary War? "I only regret that I have but one life to lose for my country." He was then promptly hanged.

Spying for a country is perhaps the most patriotic job that one can tackle. If the spy is successful, only a few will know. Even fewer will be grateful for the sacrifices he or she has made because there are bad actors posing as friends in the home government who actively work against the spy. The only time the general public reads about real spy events and escapades is when something goes very right—or very wrong. Most missions are not made public until many years later, oftentimes long after the spy has passed away from natural causes. Any news report will expose the spy and those around him or her.

Even though we know very little about what spies do in the moment, Americans are obsessed with spies. Ian Fleming, John le Carré, Robert Ludlum, Stieg Larsson, Lee Child, Graham Greene, Tom Clancy, Jason Matthews, Alistair MacLean, David Baldacci, and James Grady have all produced page-turning novels, many of which Hollywood has optioned to become blockbuster movies for those who would rather watch than read. Even though male authors dominate the spy novel world, in reality spies come in all genders.

Perhaps the allure is that spies live on the edge. We all like to think that we have an inner spy—that we too could use the tradecraft of spies to liberate sensitive information and deliver it back to our country. Of course, it is easier and safer to read a book or watch a movie. We can still be heroes in our own minds. Mix a drink and cue the music in your mind!

James M. Olson served thirty-one years in the Central Intelligence Agency (CIA), rising to the office of chief of CIA Counterintelligence before accepting an appointment to the faculty at the Bush School of Government and Public Service at Texas A&M University. Olson is the author of *Fair Play: The Moral Dilemmas of Spying.* He also developed what he called the Ten Commandments of Counterintelligence. Each rule can be adapted for fans of public houses and modern speakeasies as rules to remember when imbibing. Olson's commandments are in bold with my commentary following.

RULES FOR DRINKING COCKTAILS LIKE A SPY
ADAPTED FROM THE TEN COMMANDMENTS OF COUNTERINTELLIGENCE

Be offensive The best defense is a good offense. When drinking, make sure that you have your end game in mind so that you do not violate the law.

Honor your professionals Bartenders and servers work hard, and most don't receive the respect that they should. Honor your professional bartender and server; give generous tips for good service.

Own the street Know the bars in your area, know the bartenders, and know their best cocktails.

Know your history Read David Wondrich, Michael Veach, Iain Gately, Wayne Curtis, Ted Haigh, and others so that you know the stories behind the drinks you order.

Do not ignore analysis Trends change, but you should always be able to tell a good cocktail.

Do not be parochial A bar is a good place to have fun, but don't have that fun at someone else's expense, especially the bartender or server. Open your mind to new cocktails.

Train your people Make sure your friends know how to make and order cocktails. Or if you are a bartender or server, make sure that the people you work with know how to make cocktails.

Do not be shoved aside Be nice, but make sure that you are able to get your order in to the bartender or the server.

Do not stay too long Make sure that you know your limits. No one likes to deal with someone who is intoxicated.

Never give up Bartenders keep making great cocktails, so keep looking for great, innovative cocktails.

MODERN RULES FOR MAKING COCKTAILS LIKE A SPY

Have one or more aliases The best way to avoid being detected is to use an alias or two . . . or three. Just make sure you know your backstory.

Use and respect codenames Adding a codename adds to your mystique. Thanks to movies and books, almost any codename will add to your credibility. You might consider numbers, letters, or a simple name. Don't rule anything out.

Know your brands Spies know their brands. They don't have time to waste when ordering a drink. You should also know your brand when ordering a drink.

Know your drinks You can start off small on this one and learn new ones all the time. An old-fashioned, a Manhattan, a martini, or a gin and tonic will get you started. Learn as many drinks as you can, and be prepared to match a drink to a situation.

Dress for success A real spy should look good. Men should have a good suit that fits well. Ladies should have a nice dress that fits well.

Call your drinks A real spy calls the brand that he or she enjoys. Know what kind of whiskey you want in your Manhattan or what kind of vodka or gin you want in your martini. Spies are masters at making decisions. They are not afraid to ask for what they enjoy drinking.

Pay with cash If you are trying to stay off the grid, pay with cash. Bartenders and servers prefer cash, so you can keep them happy.

Don't draw attention to yourself Blend in and try to avoid unneeded attention at all costs. It is best to slip in and out of a bar without drawing attention to yourself.

Never let a friend drive intoxicated Never let your friend drive intoxicated. A secret mission will come to an end quickly if you or your friends are intoxicated behind the wheel.

Don't drive intoxicated Don't blow your cover and expose your team by driving intoxicated.

For those who plan to create their own bars at home or for those who already have bars, you might consider checking or double-checking to make sure that you have the following items to maximize your and your guests' experience.

MENU

Write a menu of the drinks you feel confident making when your friends visit. Make sure these are drinks you can produce quickly and with little effort so that you don't spend time flipping through books. For example, David A. Embury, the author of *The Fine Art of Mixing Drinks*, which was published in 1948, writes that the average host "can get along very nicely" knowing how to make six good cocktails. He suggests the gin martini, the Manhattan, the old-fashioned, the daiquiri, the sidecar, and the Jack Rose, all of which still work almost fourscore years later. Start small and simple with one drink. Once you have perfected the one, set a goal for five drinks; then you can expand to ten drinks as you learn them and set the goal of twenty drinks later. Spend time studying drinks away from the bar so that you can build your menu. A menu will keep you focused and will keep your inventory small and focused too. The more drinks you add to that list, the more inventory you will need on hand so that you can produce those drinks.

SETTING THE BAR

Make sure you have the correct equipment for your bar. You might include one or more of each of the following pieces of equipment. Spies are confident and always have the correct tools for the job. They come to the job prepared.

Bar mat Bar mats come in assorted sizes and colors, which means you can look for the perfect mat to match your bar or the decor of your home. Bar mats provide a stable, slip-free place to mix drinks. Also, they will contain spills and protect the surface below the mat.

Barspoon The barspoon is one of the most important tools of a bartender. Generally, the barspoon is a very long spoon, about eleven inches, with a twisted handle with a spoon at one end and a disk at the other. The twisted handle aids the bartender in stirring a drink in a mixing glass. The disk can be used to muddle soft items in the bottom of the glass and can be used to layer different alcohols in a glass for a classic layered drink.

Blender Every house and bar should have a blender, no matter what you think of blended drinks. There are some drinks that really should be blended. If you are going to use a blender, make sure to use ice that is already crushed to ensure you add years to the blades and the overall life of the blender. Examples of blended drinks include the margarita, the piña colada, and daiquiris.

Channel knife A channel knife is a small tool that helps the bartender create citrus twists. The blade of the tool cuts perfect twists both short and long to garnish drinks.

Citrus squeezer Fresh fruit juice makes a cocktail. The citrus squeezer is a tool that comes in numerous sizes specifically for limes, lemons, and other citrus fruits such as oranges and grapefruit. The tool acts as a lever that closes around the fruit, squeezing the juice out of the fruit.

Corkscrew A good corkscrew is important to have on hand to remove corks and bottle caps from bottles. The twisted "worm" is inserted into the cork to grab the cork for removal.

Ice Ice is a tool as well as part of the drink. Ice helps cool the drink quickly as well as chill the glass. Ice comes in diverse sizes and shapes. Bartenders should choose the ice size and shape based on the drink being created. Generally, ice comes in three shapes: cubed, crushed, and shaved. Today, there are many choices for molds and cut ice.

Ice scoop Ice should always be scooped into a glass. An ice scoop is a handled scoop that allows the bartender to effortlessly move ice from the ice bin to the mixing glass or to the drinking glass.

Jigger A jigger is a small two-sided hourglass-shaped measuring cup used to quickly and accurately measure out various portions of liquor, liqueur, juice, and other liquids to make cocktails. Most common jiggers are 1 ½ ounces on the large side and 1 ounce or less on the small side.

Julep strainer The julep strainer is a curved plate strainer made from stainless steel that is used to strain drinks from the mixing glass when there is no need for a fine strain.

Knife and cutting board A sharp paring knife should always be part of a properly equipped bar. Knives are used to cut fruit and make garnishes. The cutting board should be small, just large enough to hold a piece of fruit.

Muddler A muddler is a small bat-shaped stick of wood or rod of metal. The muddler is used to crush sugar cubes and citrus fruits so they can be incorporated into the drink.

Napkins Napkins add a little class to the drink and will collect any condensation on the outside of the glass so that it does not damage the surface on which the glass is sitting. The color and design of the napkin can coordinate or contrast with the bar.

Pour spout For a professional-looking bar, each bottle should be outfitted with a pour spout. This tool allows the bartender to create a consistent flow of liquid from any bottle. This reliable flow allows the bartender to reduce waste when pouring drinks.

Shaker Bartenders use two distinct types of shakers: the Boston shaker and the cobbler shaker. The Boston shaker comes in two parts: the tin and the mixing glass. If you use a Boston shaker, you will also need to purchase a strainer to hold the ice in the glass when straining the drink into the glass. The cobbler shaker is a self-contained shaker, tin, and strainer all in one.

Small mesh strainer A small mesh strainer is used to strain out small chips of ice from a drink that is already being strained from a mixing glass or shaker. Sometimes this is referred to as the double strain.

Strainer A drink should always be served over fresh ice, which means a drink that is mixed or shaken should be strained from the mixing glass or the shaker into a glass that contains fresh ice. For a drink that is served straight up, the drink should be strained into a glass that has been chilled with a mixture of ice cubes and water.

Straws Bartenders use straws as tools in several ways. The straw can be a usable garnish for a drink. The straw gives the drink a finished look and provides the guest a way to sip the drink without touching his or her lips to the side of the glass. The other use for a straw is for sampling the drink. The bartender can dip the straw into the drink and then put a finger over the top of the straw to create a vacuum that will hold the liquid. The bartender can then taste the drink through the open end of the straw. Many bartenders use this technique to make sure that the balance of the drink is correct and that the drink tastes the way it should.

Swizzle sticks Swizzle sticks are used for built drinks, especially drinks from the Caribbean. The swizzle stick is used to mix the drink.

INGREDIENTS

Vodka Vodka is non-aged, clear, distilled spirit with no aroma and no flavor. Vodka can be made from almost anything with sugar. Bartenders like vodka because this neutral spirit sells well and mixes into drinks like a dream.

Gin Gin is a non-aged, clear, distilled spirit with a very distinct flavor and aroma. Gin starts off as a neutral spirit. Each gin is different, but most will have juniper berry in the flavor and aroma. Many mixed drinks are made with gin.

Rum Rum is a distilled spirit that can be non-aged or aged. Made from sugarcane, rum is an excellent mixer.

Tequila Tequila is a distilled spirit that can be non-aged or aged. This spirit is made from the agave plant. Unlike all the other spirits that are made from the annual crops of the world, tequila's agave takes almost a decade to grow. Great planning goes into tequila's production.

Brandy Brandy is a distilled spirit that can be non-aged or aged. Brandy is made from fruit wine, in most cases grape wine. Many popular brandies are aged in casks that give a golden color to the brandy.

Whiskey Whiskey is a distilled spirit that can be non-aged or aged. Whiskey is made from grain beer. All types of grains are used to make whiskey, although certain whiskeys require specific grains.

Liqueurs A liqueur is a sweetened, flavored spirit that is often used as a mixer, although liqueurs can be consumed by themselves before or after a meal. Flavors vary; fruits, nuts, and herbs make up most of the liqueurs on the market.

Fortified wine Fortified wine is wine with brandy added to raise the alcohol content. Originally added for storage and shipping, the increased alcohol also makes a terrific addition to a cocktail.

Fresh juice Cocktails are better with fresh-squeezed juice. Most cocktails that feature juice contain a citrus juice: lime, lemon, orange, or grapefruit. Make sure you have enough to make cocktails for your party. Make sure that cocktails with juice are shaken.

Garnishes Most cocktails have prescriptive garnishes. For example, the Tom Collins always comes with an orange slice and a cocktail cherry, which is the same garnish as for the old-fashioned. The Manhattan is garnished with a cocktail cherry, and the horse's neck comes with a long lemon twist. Make sure you know the proper garnishes and have plenty of garnishes for your party.

Some of the recipes you will make will call for simple syrup, which is simple and cheap to make. Some recipes call for sugar and water, but simple syrup will save time and will ensure that the sugar is completely dissolved. Here is a recipe for a good simple syrup to make at home.

Homemade Simple Syrup

Yield: about 2 cups
1 cup water
1 ½ cups sugar

Place both the water and the sugar into a small pot. Bring the mixture to a boil for three minutes; then take the resulting syrup off the heat and let cool. Put the syrup into a plastic bottle and use as needed.

Anytime a drink calls for lime juice or lemon juice and simple syrup, you can substitute sour mix. For example, if the drink calls for 1 ounce of lemon juice and ½ ounce simple syrup, then 1 ½ ounces of sour mix can be used instead. The following is a good sour mix to use at a home bar and builds on the knowledge of making simple syrup.

Homemade Sour Mix

1 ½ cups sugar
1 cup water
1 cup fresh-squeezed lemon juice
½ cup fresh-squeezed lime juice
½ cup fresh-squeezed orange juice

Squeeze enough lemons, limes, and oranges to have the needed quantity of juice. Mix the juices together and refrigerate. Make the simple syrup with the sugar and the water by boiling for three minutes. Cool the simple syrup; then add to the fresh-squeezed juice.

Grenadine is a sweet and tart syrup used to flavor and color drinks a shade of red or pink. The origin of the word *grenadine* comes from French word *grenade*, which means *pomegranate*. This is an easy recipe to make and will elevate drinks beyond the store-bought version.

HOMEMADE GRENADINE

Yield: 2 cups
1 cup pomegranate juice (no sugar added)
1 ½ cups sugar
½ teaspoon fresh lemon juice

Pour the sugar and the pomegranate juice into a pot. Warm, stirring the whole time, until the sugar dissolves into the juice. Pull from heat and allow to cool. Once cool, add the lemon juice. Store in bottles or jars under refrigeration. Use as needed.

There are some very good cocktail cherries on the market. If cherries are in season, you might try making them yourself. Here is an easy recipe that will get you started.

HOMEMADE COCKTAIL CHERRIES

40 fresh cherries
¼ teaspoon cinnamon
2 cups plus ¼ cup bourbon (or your favorite spirit)

Pit the cherries. Heat a pan on the stove, pour the cherries into the pan, and sauté in the ¼ cup bourbon. If the cherries catch the flame, remove from the stove until the flame burns out. Add the cinnamon and mix. Pour the cherries into a sanitized jar and cover with bourbon. Allow to cool and refrigerate. Serve with your favorite cocktail that calls for a cocktail cherry.

Homemade Orgeat Syrup

1 cup almond milk
1 cup simple syrup
1 teaspoon orange flower water
1 ounce bourbon

Mix the almond milk and simple syrup together. Add the bourbon and orange flower water, stir together, and then let sit for twenty-four hours. Use as directed in cocktails.

GLASSWARE

Champagne flute A champagne flute is a tall drink glass designed to hold sparkling wine. With a narrow opening at the top, the glass effectively holds the CO_2 and releases the gas slowly, which allows for tiny streams of bubbles floating to the top of the glass. This glass is great for many cocktails, including the Seelbach cocktail and the French 75.

Cocktail glass Also known as a martini glass, this is the perfect vessel for a chilled drink served straight up. The V-shaped glass is iconic.

Highball glass Perfect for long drinks, this tall glass holds ice as well as at least ten ounces of liquid.

Hurricane glass This is an hourglass-shaped glass used for the hurricane cocktail and other drinks.

Margarita glass A glass specifically for the margarita, it has a large flat bowl at the top.

Mug This is a large vessel used for beer and cocktails.

Mule mug This distinctive copper mug is traditionally used for the mule family of drinks.

Old-fashioned A glass with straight sides and a flat bottom, it is also known as a low-ball glass or a rocks glass.

Pilsner glass The pilsner glass is perfect for a glass of beer or for a beer cocktail.

Pint glass The pint glass is used for beer and other cocktails.

Red wine glass This is a wine glass with a large bowl on top and a long stem.

Shot glass This small glass holds between 1 and 2 ounces or a shot of spirits.

White wine glass This is a wine glass with a small bowl on top and a long stem.

Bartenders use several techniques to make drinks properly. Each drink calls for a specific technique. Knowing how to complete drinks using these techniques will increase street credibility for the home bartender.

TECHNIQUES

Blending Using the blending technique is important for blended drinks such as the blended margarita, daiquiri, or piña colada. Blending is important for incorporating thick dairy products and whole or frozen fruit. Try to use less ice; too much ice will water down the finished drink. A happy medium is to use some ice and frozen fruit to maximize the flavor of the drink. Crushed ice should always be used for this technique to help extend the life and blades of the blender. When using crushed ice, be sure to blend for twenty seconds, stop, then blend for ten seconds.

Building Building a drink is simply pouring one ingredient into the glass after another until all the ingredients are in the glass. This technique is used for gin and tonics, Moscow mules, Collinses, and screwdrivers.

Layering The layering technique involves the bartender's knowledge of the specific gravity of a liquid. The heavier liquids are used as a base, while the lighter liquids are floated (or layered) on top of the heavier liquids to create a layered appearance in the glass. Examples of layered drinks include the B-52, the tequila sunrise, the black and tan, and the classic pousse-café.

Muddling The technique of muddling is highlighted by the bartender's use of a muddler to crush sugar, citrus fruit, or herbs before adding ice and alcohol to the drink. Generally, the herb or fruit should be lightly muddled so as not to release bitter flavors of overmuddled items. The old-fashioned, caipirinha, mint julep, and mojito are examples of muddled drinks.

Shaking The shaking method is used for drinks that need to combine ingredients that might not easily combine in a uniform manner any other way. Shaking will also aerate the cocktail, allowing for a foam or froth on top of the cocktail. Cocktails with citrus juice or egg whites are typically shaken cocktails. Examples of cocktails that use the shaking method are the cosmopolitan, the kamikaze, and the sidecar.

Stirring Stirring is perfect for drinks that are completely made from alcoholic beverages. The purpose of stirring the drink is to make sure that you have a result that is crystal clear. To complete this technique, fill a mixing glass with ice, and then pour the ingredients into the glass. Using a barspoon, stir the drink at least forty turns or until completely chilled. Top the mixing glass with a strainer, and pour the drink into a chilled glass or a glass with ice. The Manhattan, negroni, and martini are examples of stirred cocktails.

COCKTAIL CREATION: A BALANCING ACT

Keep in mind that cocktail creation is a balancing act. A great cocktail is not too sweet, not too sour, and not too bitter. The perfect cocktail is just right. When you see a bartender stick a straw into a drink to syphon out a sip of the cocktail, the bartender is checking for balance in flavor.

A great cocktail to play with is the old-fashioned. The home bartender can play around with the recipe to see how each of the elements plays a part in the overall cocktail creation. In the case of the old-fashioned, the sugar melts into the water and provides the sweet element to the cocktail. Bitters are added to help elevate the flavor of the cocktail and to counter the sugar so that the drink is not too sweet. The spirit is added and brings the cocktail together. But wait—what type of spirit? Each spirit will have a different reaction to the overall recipe. The old-fashioned will have a different balance and different flavor based on the spirit.

Another cocktail that the home bartender can play around with is the homemade margarita. This is a splendid example of a "sour" drink. We want the margarita to be sour but not too sour, which is why we balance the drink with sweet—but not too much. This balance in flavor is important.

In my head, I think I'd make a perfect spy,
but in reality, I don't think I'd fare
very well. —Matthew Rhys

I was never a spy. I was with the OSS organization.
We had a number of women, but we were
all office help. —Julia Child

Cocktail Recipes

A GOOD SPY OPERATES WITHOUT detection. Like a good spy, the genesis of all alcoholic beverages is a near invisible process, fermentation. During fermentation, yeast converts sugar into alcohol and carbon dioxide. Fermentation creates both beer and wine. Beer is made from a liquid laced primarily with grains such as barley, rice, and corn. Wine is made from the liquids from fruit. Fermented beverages such as beer and wine can be served in cocktails, but they can also be distilled into spirits at a higher alcohol by volume.

Spirits fall into three categories: (1) clear spirits; (2) spirits that are sometimes clear and sometimes brown; and (3) brown spirits. Each of the spirit categories is represented in this chapter. First are the clear spirits, vodka and gin. Then are the spirits that come both clear and brown, rum and tequila (and mescal), followed by the brown spirits, brandy and whiskey. Finally, there are other cocktails that are made with wine, beer, or liqueurs.

Vodka is the choice of James Bond for martinis—shaken, not stirred. Vodka is the perfect spirit for a spy and for a bartender, albeit for different reasons. Vodka is colorless and flavorless and has little aroma; in other words, the spirit is neutral once it is mixed into a cocktail, which allows maximum creativity from the bartender and maximum discretion for the spy. This lack of distinguishable character arises from distilling vodka to higher alcohol by volume and then watering it down to the desired proof. Smirnoff capitalized on this in 1953, creating an ad campaign: "It leaves you breathless!" The campaign was a play on words. The vodka is undetectable when mixed with other beverages such as orange juice, tomato juice, or tonic water. Most other spirits can be detected on the breath of the person consuming that spirit.

VODKA COCKTAILS

Vodka can be made from anything, but most are made from grains or potatoes. Today, vodka is one of the most popular spirits with bar customers. Bartenders love it too because, as many bartenders will tell you, "Vodka pays the bills."

Perhaps no cocktail is more synonymous with spies or secret agents than the vodka martini, which is sometimes known as the vodkatini. James Bond calls for a dry vodka martini—shaken, not stirred—in many movies. This is a basic recipe that all bartenders, home and professional, should know by heart. A wonderful aspect of this cocktail is all of the decisions one can make when ordering such a simple drink. Vodka or gin? Shaken or stirred? Lemon peel or olives for garnish? Each decision changes the drink slightly.

MARTINI
(VODKA VERSUS GIN; SHAKEN VERSUS STIRRED)

½ ounce dry vermouth
2 ounces vodka
1, 2, or 3 stuffed green olives or lemon peel
Ice

Fill a cocktail glass with ice and water to chill the glass. Fill a mixing glass with ice. Add the vermouth and vodka to the mixing glass. Stir until the combination is cold, about forty stirs. Discard the ice and water in the cocktail glass. Strain the martini into the cocktail glass and garnish with one or more olives or lemon peel. Serve.

Note: If you want to shake this drink, you can—just set the shaker up with ice and follow the recipe substituting shaking for stirring. Also, look for different types of stuffing in your olives, such as blue cheese, almonds, pimentos, or garlic.

A spymaster is someone who runs or leads a spy ring or agency. There are many examples of spymasters, but perhaps none was as elusive and at the same time famous as Markus "Mischa" Wolf. Wolf was the spymaster's spymaster. He was known by many as "the man without a face" because most agencies did not know what he looked like. Wolf was the director of East Germany's Ministry for State Security, or Stasi, directing thousands of spies. Spy novelist John le Carré denied multiple times that Wolf served as the inspiration for the fictional Russian spymaster Karla in his George Smiley series. Wolf was the author of *Man without a Face: The*

Autobiography of Communism's Greatest Spymaster. When Wolf died in 2006 at the age of eighty-three, his obituary was featured in the *New York Times*, and le Carré again denied Wolf served as an inspiration. This cocktail is named for the idea of a spymaster.

SPYMASTER

1 ½ ounces vodka
½ ounce crème de banana
½ ounce fresh-squeezed lemon juice
1 ounce egg white
Lemon twist

Fill an old-fashioned glass with ice and water to chill the glass. Add the vodka, crème de banana, lemon juice, and egg white to a mixing glass and close the glass with the shaking tin for a dry shake. This will allow the egg white to foam. Open the shaker, add ice, and reshake the drink. Empty the old-fashioned glass, then add ice. Strain the drink into the old-fashioned glass. Garnish with a lemon twist and serve.

Tony Mendez is a spy of the highest order. Working for the CIA in the late 1970s, Mendez partnered with Hollywood makeup artist John Chambers to create a fake movie, *Argo*. The two—with an assist from makeup artist Robert Sidell and his wife, Andi—pulled off what is now known as the Canadian Caper. During the Iran hostage crisis, six US diplomats sought sanctuary in the Canadian Embassy. Mendez organized the mission, disguised as the movie *Argo*, that helped smuggle out the six diplomats to great fanfare. Only in 1997, when the files related to the case were declassified, did the world understand Mendez and Chambers's full actions; both received awards from the CIA. Ben Affleck directed, produced, and starred in the 2012 movie *Argo*, which won Best Picture at the Eighty-Fifth Academy Awards. Affleck played Mendez, and John Goodman played John Chambers in a star-studded cast that included Bryan Cranston and Alan Arkin. The True Story cocktail was inspired by the story of *Argo*, and this is my adaptation.

TRUE STORY

2 ounces orange-flavored vodka
2 ½ ounces pink grapefruit juice
1 ounce maraschino liqueur
1 dash Dale DeGroff's Pimento Bitters
Grapefruit twist
Ice

Fill a cocktail glass with ice and water to chill the glass. Fill the tin side of a Boston shaker with ice. Add the orange-flavored vodka, grapefruit juice, maraschino liqueur, and Dale DeGroff's bitters to the glass side of the shaker, then pour the liquid into the tin and attach the two sides. Shake until the combination is cold. Discard the ice and water in the cocktail glass. Strain the True Story into the cocktail glass, then garnish with a grapefruit twist. Serve.

Sir Kingsley Amis, CBE, was a British novelist, a fan of the Bond series, and a close friend to Ian Fleming. Amis is the author of *Colonel Sun*, the first Bond book published after Ian Fleming's death. Amis wrote the novel under the pen name Robert Markham. Before authoring *Colonel Sun*, Amis authored *The James Bond Dossier*, which was the first literary study of the character, and *The Book of Bond, or Every Man His Own 007* under the pen name Lt. Col. William "Bill" Tanner. Lt. Col. Tanner is M's chief of staff in the Bond series. Amis was also a keen drinker, cocktail connoisseur, and author of *Everyday Drinking*. In this last text, he gives a recipe for the Lucky Jim, named for his first novel, *Lucky Jim*. Amis uses a 15:1 formula of vodka to vermouth similar to a Montgomery martini, which is made with gin. The Montgomery is named for Field Marshal Bernard "Monty" Montgomery, First Viscount Montgomery of Alamein. Ernest Hemingway refers to Montgomery cocktails in *Across the River and into the Trees*. Many see Hemingway's reference as a critique of Monty's command style—only attack when you outnumber the enemy 15:1 or more. When making the Lucky Jim, Amis notes to use cheap "British vodka, the cheapest you can find" and not to "waste your Russian or Polish vodka."

THE LUCKY JIM VERSUS THE MONTGOMERY

2 ounces vodka
⅛ ounce dry vermouth
¼ ounce cucumber juice
Cucumber slice
Ice

Fill a cocktail glass with ice and water to chill the glass. Fill a mixing glass with ice. Add the vodka, vermouth, and cucumber juice to the mixing glass. Stir until the combination is cold, about forty stirs. Discard the ice and water in the cocktail glass. Strain the Lucky Jim into the cocktail glass, then float the cucumber slice on top. Serve.

Each James Bond movie has a different Bond girl. Barbara Bach played Major Anya Amasova (a.k.a. Agent XXX) in *The Spy Who Loved Me* opposite Sir Roger Moore, KBE, who played Bond. Bach would go on to play a World War II spy/soldier, Maritza Petrovic, in the movie *Force 10 from Navarone*, adapted from Alistair MacLean's book by the same name. It featured Harrison Ford as Lt. Col. Mike Barnsby and Robert Shaw as Maj. Keith Mallory. Bach is now also known as Lady Starkey, a courtesy title as the wife of Sir Richard Starkey, who is better known as Ringo Starr from the Beatles.

BARBARA

1 ounce vodka
1 ounce coffee liqueur
1 ounce cream
Nutmeg
Ice

Fill a cocktail glass with ice and water to chill the glass. Fill the tin side of a Boston shaker with ice. Add the vodka, coffee liqueur, and cream to the glass side of the shaker, then pour the liquid into the tin and attach the two sides. Shake until

the combination is cold. Discard the ice and water in the
cocktail glass. Strain the cocktail into the cocktail glass and
garnish with nutmeg. Serve.

The caipirinha is a fantastic Brazilian cocktail made with cachaça, which is similar to rum, as it is a distilled spirit made from fermented sugarcane juice. By Brazilian law, only the lime version of this drink can be called a caipirinha. When vodka replaces cachaça, the cocktail becomes a caipirovska. Spies need to know how to adapt in case they find themselves without all the proper equipment regardless if they are on a case or in a bar.

Caipirovska

2 ounces vodka
1 whole lime, diced
⅓ ounce fresh lime juice
2 teaspoons sugar
Ice

Fill an old-fashioned glass with the diced lime and sugar.
Muddle the lime and sugar together. Add the vodka and lime
juice. Fill the glass with ice and stir. Garnish with a lime.
Serve.

Headquartered at the J. Edgar Hoover Building in Washington, DC, the Federal Bureau of Investigation (FBI) is the domestic intelligence service of the United States. This cocktail celebrates the FBI with a delightful mixture of ice cream, vodka, cream, and coffee liqueurs.

FBI

2 ounces vodka
1 ounce bourbon cream or Irish cream liqueur
1 ounce coffee liqueur
¼ cup vanilla ice cream
Ice

Add the ice cream to a blender. Pour the vodka, cream, and coffee liqueurs on top of the ice cream and add ice. Blend until smooth, then pour into a glass. Serve with a straw.

With a name like the Kurrant Affair, this cocktail sounds like an espionage case. This is an easy-drinking cocktail, so be careful if you are going to enjoy a Kurrant Affair—without intent, you may get into trouble.

KURRANT AFFAIR

1 ounce black currant–flavored vodka
1 ounce lemon-flavored vodka
4 ounces apple juice

Add ice and water to a highball glass to chill the glass. Add ice to the tin side of a Boston shaker. In the mixing glass, add both vodkas and the apple juice. Pour the contents of the mixing glass into the iced tin and secure the glass to the tin. Shake the contents until you hear the ice change and the contents are cold. Open the Boston shaker. Empty the highball glass, add new ice, then strain the contents of the shaker into the empty glass. Serve.

Spies have used sex for years with the intent of what follows—pillow talk. Both men and women have used or been the victims of sex in the world of espionage. Male spies who seduce targets are called ravens, while women are called swallows. The 2013 novel *Red Sparrow*, by Jason Matthews, covers this aspect of espionage. A movie by the same name starred Jennifer Lawrence in the lead role.

Pillow Talk

1 ounce strawberry- or raspberry-flavored vodka
1 ounce white chocolate–flavored liqueur
Whipped cream

Chill a shot glass. Pour the vodka into the glass. Using the back of a barspoon, carefully pour the liqueur so that the liqueur floats on top of the vodka. Top with whipped cream and serve.

Former MI6 intelligence officer and British author David John Moore Cornwell is better known by his penname, John le Carré. He started writing while he was still working for

MI6. But with the international success of his third novel, *The Spy Who Came in from the Cold*, his cover was blown, and he started writing full time. Many of his books have become movies, including the one listed above, along with *Tinker Tailor Soldier Spy*, *The Night Manager*, and *The Constant Gardener*. This cocktail named for the espionage novelist has the addition of caraway seed–flavored kümmel.

LE CARRÉ

1 ½ ounces vodka
2 splashes dry vermouth
2 splashes kümmel

Add ice and water into a cocktail glass to chill the glass. Add ice to a cocktail shaker or to the tin side of a Boston shaker. Add the vodka, vermouth, and kümmel to the mixing glass. Pour the contents of the mixing glass into the tin and make sure the two sides are attached tightly. Shake until you hear the ice change. Open the Boston shaker and pull the mixing glass side off. Empty the cocktail glass and strain the drink into the chilled cocktail glass. Serve.

The fifth novel in the James Bond series by Ian Fleming is *From Russia with Love*. Anistatia Miller and Jared Brown created a vodka-forward twist on the Vesper martini in their book *Shaken Not Stirred: A Celebration of the Martini* called From Russia with Love. The following is my adaptation of their recipe.

From Russia with Love

2 ounces vodka
1 ounce Gordon's gin
½ ounce Kina Lillet
Lemon twist or thin lemon slice

Add ice and water into a cocktail glass to chill the glass. Add ice to a cocktail shaker or to tin side of a Boston shaker. Add the vodka, Gordon's gin, and Kina Lillet to the mixing glass. Pour the contents of the mixing glass into the tin and make sure the two sides are attached tightly. Shake until you hear the ice change. Open the Boston shaker and pull the mixing glass side off. Empty the cocktail glass and strain the drink into the chilled cocktail glass. Garnish with a lemon twist or a lemon slice and serve.

During the height of the Cold War between the West and the East, the Soviet Union, or Union of Soviet Socialist Republics (USSR), was clearly on the East's side of the conflict. The United States was clearly on the West's side. This recipe for the Soviet cocktail documents their influence during this period of time.

Soviet

2 ounces vodka
¼ ounce dry vermouth
¼ ounce dry sherry

Add ice and water to a cocktail glass to chill the glass. Add ice to a mixing glass and then the vodka, vermouth, and sherry. Stir at least forty times. Then empty the chilled glass. Strain the mixture into the glass. Serve.

British actress Gemma Arterton joined an exclusive group of actresses in 2008 when she starred opposite Daniel Craig in *Quantum of Solace.* Arterton played MI6 agent Strawberry Fields, for which she won the Empire Award for Best Newcomer.

Strawberry Fields

2 strawberries
1 ½ ounces vodka
½ ounce lime juice
½ ounce simple syrup
½ ounce egg white
Strawberry for garnish

Add ice and water to a cocktail glass to chill the glass. Add ice to the tin side of a Boston shaker. Muddle the strawberries in the bottom of the mixing glass. Add to the mixing glass simple syrup, lime juice, vodka, and egg white. Pour the contents of the mixing glass into the iced tin and secure the glass to the tin. Shake the contents until the ice sounds different and the contents are cold. Open the Boston shaker. Empty the cocktail glass, then strain the contents of the shaker into the empty glass. Garnish with a strawberry. Serve.

Col. Rudolf Able was a Soviet intelligence officer who was caught in the United States and charged with espionage. He was offered the chance to work for the United States as a double agent but turned the offer down. Able was convicted and sentenced to thirty years in prison. Eventually he was traded for American Gary Powers.

Kremlin Colonel

2 ounces vodka
⅔ ounce lime juice
⅔ ounce simple syrup
4 sprigs of mint
Mint bud

Add ice and water to a cocktail glass to chill the glass. Add ice to the tin side of a Boston shaker. Add to the mixing glass simple syrup, lime juice, vodka, and mint sprigs. Pour the contents of the mixing glass into the iced tin and secure the glass to the tin. Shake the contents until the ice sounds different and the contents are cold. Open the Boston shaker. Empty the cocktail glass, then strain the contents of the shaker into the empty glass. Garnish with the mint bud. Serve.

GIN COCKTAILS

Gin starts as a neutral spirit, similar to vodka, but the spirit is exposed to a brand-specific proprietary mixture of seeds, roots, barks, herbs, and spices, with the most common being juniper berries. Gin remains a clear spirit. Many excellent cocktails rely on gin's specific flavor.

Ian Fleming invented the Vesper martini in his first novel, *Casino Royale*. Bond asks for a "dry martini" served "in a deep champagne goblet," then addresses the French bartender calling for "three measures of Gordons, one of vodka, half measure of Kina Littet." By any volume measurement system metric, imperial, or standard US, this is a huge martini, but Bond explains to his American counterpart, CIA agent Felix Leiter, "I do like that one [drink] to be very large and very strong." I have scaled this drink down because we can't all be James Bond, or Ian Fleming, for that matter. According to Bond's instructions, "Shake it very well until it's ice-cold, then add a large thin slice of lemon peel." Gordon's gin is very important for this drink, as the gin choice adds a lot of the flavor and each gin has a different flavor.

Vesper Martini

2 ounces Gordon's gin
½ ounce vodka
¼ ounce Kina Lillet
Lemon twist or thin lemon slice

Add ice and water into a cocktail glass to chill the glass. Add ice to a cocktail shaker or to tin side of a Boston shaker. Add the Gordon's gin, vodka, and Kina Lillet to the mixing glass. Pour the contents of the mixing glass into the tin and make sure the two sides are attached tightly. Shake until you hear the ice change. Open the Boston shaker and pull the mixing glass side off. Empty the cocktail glass and strain the drink into the chilled cocktail glass. Garnish with a lemon twist or a lemon slice and serve.

The opera *Tosca* proved to be the perfect place for James Bond to gather information in the movie *Quantum of Solace*. The scene opens with Bond viewing the audience from the catwalk above the stage, listening to a conversation among several people who are seated in multiple locations in the audience. As the opera progresses to a murder scene, Bond identifies and pursues the mastermind.

OPERA

2 ounces gin
1 ounce Dubonnet
½ ounce Curaçao
Orange zest spiral

Add ice to a cocktail glass and a little water to chill the glass, then set the glass aside. Add the gin, Dubonnet, and Curaçao to a mixing glass. Stir until chilled (about forty stirs). Empty the cocktail glass. Add the orange spiral to the bottom and side of the cocktail glass. Strain the mixed Opera from the mixing glass into the cocktail glass. Serve.

This next drink, the gin gimlet, is perfect for a spy because the idea is simple, although it is one of the most difficult drinks to make. There needs to be a balance between the gin, the lime, and sweetness. Too much lime, and the drink will be too tart, while not enough will make the drink too strong. Too much or too little sugar, and the drink will be unbalanced. I suggest using sweetened lime juice to help with the formula. Tastes will vary among palates, so you might need to experiment and adjust this drink a little.

Gin Gimlet

1 ½ ounces gin
½ ounce Rose's Sweetened Lime Juice
Thin slice of lime
Ice

Fill a cocktail glass with ice and water to chill the glass. Fill the tin side of a Boston shaker with ice. Add the gin and Rose's Sweetened Lime Juice to the glass side of the shaker, then pour the liquid into the tin and attach the two sides. Shake until the combination is cold. Discard the ice and water in the cocktail glass. Strain the gin gimlet into the cocktail glass, then float the lime on top. Serve.

Adm. Sir Hugh Sinclair, KCB, worked in naval intelligence at the beginning of World War I. Shortly after the Great War, he took command of British Naval Intelligence. In 1923, he was appointed the second director of the Secret Intelligence Service (SIS), which is better known as MI6, an organization that he oversaw until his death of cancer in 1939. During his tenure, there were several penetrations into MI6 by the Germans in Europe.

ADMIRAL COCKTAIL

1 ½ ounces gin
1 ounce cherry liqueur
½ ounce lime juice

Add ice and water to a cocktail glass to chill the glass. Add ice to the tin side of a Boston shaker. In the mixing glass, add the lime juice, cherry liqueur, and the gin. Pour the contents of the mixing glass into the iced tin and secure the glass to the tin. Shake the contents until the ice sounds different and the contents are cold. Open the Boston shaker. Empty the cocktail glass, then strain the contents of the shaker into the empty glass. Serve.

A spy needs to maintain good health, and the medicinal qualities of a gin and tonic can help with that. Tonic water contains quinine, which helps prevent malaria. Tonic water is bitter and pairs well with gin and lime. In any case, a fun bar trick—tonic water fluoresces under ultraviolet light—may surprise your friends.

GIN AND TONIC

2 ounces gin
4 ounces tonic water
2 slices of lime

Add ice to an old-fashioned glass. Then add the gin and top with tonic water. The carbonated tonic water will mix the drink. Garnish with lime. Serve.

Many governments have long used airplanes for espionage to drop supplies or spies into areas of conflict. Gary Powers was a pilot of a Lockheed U-2, a high-altitude reconnaissance aircraft over the Soviet Union in 1960. The U-2 was shot down. Powers was able to escape the aircraft, but the Soviets captured him and took him to Lubyanka Prison. The United States insisted that the U-2 that was shot down was actually an off-course weather plane. Eventually, Powers was exchanged for KGB officer Col. Rudolf Able, who had been caught spying in the United States for the Soviet Union. This exchange was memorialized in the Steven Spielberg movie *Bridge of Spies* starring Tom Hanks. Actor Austin Stowell played Powers. Later, the United States would award Powers some of its highest honors, including the CIA's Intelligence Star, the CIA's Director's Medal, the Silver Star, the Prisoner of War Medal, and the Distinguished Flying Cross; many of these honors were presented posthumously, as Powers died in a helicopter crash in 1977 while covering a wildfire in Santa Barbara, California, for KNBC.

AVIATION

2 ounces gin
½ ounce maraschino liqueur
½ ounce lemon juice
Cocktail cherry

Add ice and water to a cocktail glass to chill the glass. Add ice to a cocktail shaker. Add the lemon juice, maraschino liqueur, and gin to the cocktail shaker. Shake until you hear the ice change and the contents are cold. Empty the glass and strain the cocktail into the glass. Garnish with the cocktail cherry and serve.

The Adventures of Frank Race was an adventure series about an OSS officer that was aired over the radio from the late 1940s to the early 1950s. For the first twenty-two episodes, actor Tom Collins voiced the character Frank Race. The Tom Collins cocktail is basically a gin sour with soda water.

Tom Collins

2 ounces gin
1 ounce sweet and sour mixture
4 ounces soda water
Orange slice
Cocktail cherry
Ice

Prepare a Collins glass with ice to chill the glass. Add gin and sweet and sour mixture, then stir. Top with club soda and stir. Garnish with an orange slice and a cocktail cherry. Serve.

The reason spies are so careful is if they are caught, death is all but assured. While captured members of the military become prisoners of war, spies are usually executed. This cocktail is for those who like cherry flavors.

Captive

2 ounces gin
½ ounce cherry brandy
½ ounce kirschwasser

Add ice and water to a cocktail glass to chill the glass. Add ice to the tin side of a Boston shaker. In the mixing glass, add the kirschwasser, cherry brandy, and gin. Pour the contents of the mixing glass into the iced tin and secure the glass to the tin. Shake the contents until the ice sounds different and the contents are cold. Open the Boston shaker. Empty the cocktail glass, then strain the contents of the shaker into the empty glass. Serve.

Some of the best cocktails are simple and quick. Spies need simple and quick. The gin cup is easy to prepare. The mint and lemon juice complement the gin for a wonderfully refreshing spring or summer cocktail.

Gin Cup

4 sprigs mint
1 teaspoon sugar
3 ounces gin
1 ounce lemon juice
Ice

Add three sprigs of mint and sugar to an old-fashioned glass. Lightly bruise the mint with a muddler (do not crush). Add the lemon juice and stir. Add the gin and then the ice, and stir again. Take the final sprig of mint, and clap it between your hands to awaken the aroma in the mint. Garnish the drink with the mint. Serve.

From James Bond to Austin Powers, many spies have used casinos as places to conduct business and to let off a little steam. While games of chance seem counterproductive for a spy, the espionage profession does lend itself to a bit of chance with the real possibility of getting caught.

Casino

1 ½ ounces Old Tom gin
¼ ounce maraschino liqueur
¼ ounce orange bitters
¼ ounce lemon juice
Lemon twist
Cocktail cherry

Add ice and water to a cocktail glass to chill the glass. Add ice to the tin side of a Boston shaker. In the mixing glass, add the Old Tom gin, maraschino liqueur, orange bitters, and lemon juice. Pour the contents of the mixing glass into the iced tin and secure the glass to the tin. Shake the contents until the ice sounds different and the contents are cold. Open the Boston shaker. Empty the cocktail glass, then strain the contents of the shaker into the empty glass. Garnish with a lemon twist and a cocktail cherry. Serve.

The Mbolero is a great example of hidden flavors. To the eye, this cocktail appears regular enough, but hidden in the glass is a wonderful combination of mint, bitters, and gin fit for any spy.

MBOLERO

2 ounces gin
½ ounce lime juice
6 dashes orange bitters
6 mint leaves
1 dash simple syrup
Ice cubes
Small mint sprig

Add ice and water to a cocktail glass to chill the glass. In the mixing glass, add the gin, lime juice, orange bitters, mint leaves, and simple syrup. Fill the tin side of a Boston shaker with ice. Pour the contents of the mixing glass into the tin and secure the glass to the tin. Shake until the ice sounds different

and the contents are cold. Open the Boston shaker. Empty the
cocktail glass, then strain the contents of the shaker into the
empty glass. Garnish with mint sprig and serve.

Pink gin was originally a favorite with the British Royal Navy
to help with seasickness or to enjoy gin. In literature, many
spies have enjoyed this drink. British author Graham Greene
uses it in his book *The Heart of the Matter*, Ian Fleming has
James Bond order pink gin in *The Man with the Golden Gun*,
and John le Carré has Gerald Westerby order it in *Tinker Tailor Soldier Spy*.

PINK GIN

2 ounces gin
1 to 4 dashes Angostura bitters

*Add ice and water to a cocktail glass to chill the glass. Add
ice to the tin side of a Boston shaker. In the mixing glass, add
the gin and bitters. Pour the contents of the mixing glass
into the iced tin and secure the glass to the tin. Shake the
contents until the ice sounds different and the contents are
cold. Open the Boston shaker. Empty the cocktail glass, then
strain the contents of the shaker into the empty glass. Serve.*

In Paris's eighteenth arrondissement is a hill called Mont-
martre, on top of which the famous Basilica of the Sacré
Cœur (the Scared Heart) is visually recognizable. The area's

claim to fame includes the many famous artists who called this area of Paris home, such as Claude Monet, Pablo Picasso, Vincent van Gogh, and Henri de Toulouse-Lautrec, to name a few. The area has also been used in many movies, including the 1998 action movie *Ronin* starring Robert De Niro, Jean Reno, Jonathan Pryce, Sean Bean, and Stellan Skarsgård. In the movie, Sam (De Niro) is an American mercenary associated with the CIA.

MONTMARTRE

2 ounces gin
½ ounce triple sec
½ ounce sweet vermouth
Cocktail cherry

Add ice and water to a cocktail glass to chill the glass. Add ice to the tin side of a Boston shaker. In the mixing glass, add the triple sec, vermouth, and gin. Pour the contents of the mixing glass into the iced tin and secure the glass to the tin. Shake the contents until the ice sounds different and the contents are cold. Open the Boston shaker. Empty the cocktail glass, then strain the contents of the shaker into the empty glass. Garnish with a cocktail cherry. Serve.

Both West Point, the military academy for new army officers, and the Naval Academy at Annapolis have been involved in espionage—one real and one in fiction. During the Revolutionary War, Fort Arnold at West Point, New York, was almost surrendered to the British by Maj. Gen. Benedict Arnold, but the plot was foiled because of good espionage on the part of the Revolutionary cause. The fort was renamed Fort Clinton. President Thomas Jefferson ordered that the area become a military academy shortly after becoming president. As for Arnold, his name would become synonymous with treason and betrayal. Annapolis was the real set for the movie *Patriot Games*, starring Harrison Ford, Anne Archer, Sean Bean, James Earl Jones, Samuel L. Jackson, and Richard Harris. The movie is based on Tom Clancy's novel by the same name and is part of the Jack Ryan series. There are several scenes on campus or right off campus where Dr. Jack Ryan teaches in the History Department.

ARMY AND NAVY COCKTAIL

2 ounces gin
¾ ounce orgeat syrup
¾ ounce lemon juice
Cocktail cherry

Add ice and water to a cocktail glass to chill the glass. Add ice to the tin side of a Boston shaker. In the mixing glass, add the gin, orgeat syrup, and lemon juice. Pour the contents of the mixing glass into the iced tin and secure the glass to the tin. Shake the contents until the ice sounds different and the contents are cold. Open the Boston shaker. Empty the cocktail glass, then strain the contents of the shaker into the empty glass. Garnish with a cocktail cherry. Serve.

RUM COCKTAILS

Rum is made all over the world from sugar, sugarcane juice, molasses, or other sugar by-products. Rum is another bartender favorite because of the spirit's flexibility in cocktails. Rum comes in a wide spectrum of clear to brown colors, which develop based on how long the rum ages in oak barrels that have been charred on the inside. Most are distilled to a high proof and watered down to a market 80 proof (40 percent alcohol by volume). Some rum is sold at a higher "over-proof" 151 proof (75.5 percent alcohol by volume).

Austin Powers became a household name in the late 1990s as a trilogy of films featuring the British spy in a spoof of James Bond and 1960s and 1970s spy movies. The legendary Burt Bacharach makes a cameo appearance in each Austin Powers movie. Bacharach composed the soundtrack for the 1967 movie *Casino Royale* starring David Niven as 007. Bacharach was nominated for an Academy Award for the song "The Look of Love." Powers, a Mike Myers creation, was introduced with *Austin Powers: International Man of Mystery*, followed by *Austin Powers: The Spy Who Shagged Me*, and *Goldmember*. There are rumors of a fourth installment in this franchise. Each film features an amazing soundtrack, and each has included "Soul Bossa Nova," by Grammy and Tony Award winner Quincy Jones.

BOSSANOVA

2 ounces white rum
½ ounce Galliano
½ ounce apricot brandy
4 ounces apple juice
1 ounce lime juice
½ ounce simple syrup
Lime wheel or lime wedge
Ice

Add ice and water to a highball glass to chill the glass. Add ice to the tin side of a Boston shaker. In the mixing glass, add the rum, Galliano, apricot brandy, apple juice, lime juice, and simple syrup. Pour the contents of the mixing glass into the iced tin and secure the glass to the tin. Shake the contents until the ice sounds different and the contents are cold. Open the Boston shaker. Empty the highball glass, refill with ice, and then strain the contents of the shaker into the glass. Garnish with a lime wheel or wedge. Serve.

The island of St. Lucia looks like one of the glamorous, picturesque locations where a spy film might be filmed. The blue water, sandy beaches, and charming venues give this member of the British Commonwealth all of the ingredients for an exceptional location for any movie, especially an espionage film.

St. Lucia

2 ounces rum (white or golden)
1 ounce dry vermouth
1 ounce triple sec or Curaçao
2 ounces orange juice
1 teaspoon grenadine
Cocktail cherry
Orange twist

Add ice and water to a highball glass to chill the glass. Add ice to the tin side of a Boston shaker. In the mixing glass, add the rum, vermouth, triple sec, orange juice, and grenadine. Pour the contents of the mixing glass into the iced tin and secure the glass to the tin. Shake the contents until the ice sounds different and the contents are cold. Open the Boston shaker. Empty the highball glass, refill with ice, and then strain the contents of the shaker into the glass. Garnish with the orange twist and cocktail cherry. Serve.

Betsy Flanagan is a popular character in cocktail lore and early America. She lived in and ran a tavern in the town of Elmsford, New York, during the Revolutionary War. She is credited with creating the term *cocktail* for her French and American guests. According to the story, Betsy would steal roosters from her neighbor, who was loyal to King George III. She would cook the rooster (or cock) into stew or soup for the troops and guests. Then she would use the tail feathers as drink stirrers. Thus the cocktail was born. Flanagan's support for the revolutionary cause would have made her a traitor to the king's forces. Some of the guests at Flanagan's tavern might have been spies. The Betsy Flanagan is a very ironic cocktail because it features rum and looks more like a Manhattan. Replace the rum with rye or bourbon for a Manhattan, or Scotch for a Rob Roy, and eliminate the simple syrup.

BETSY FLANAGAN VERSUS THE MANHATTAN (OR ROB ROY)

2 ounces Jamaican rum
1 ounce sweet vermouth
1 or 2 dashes Angostura bitters
½ teaspoon simple syrup
Cocktail cherry

Add ice and water to a cocktail glass to chill the glass. Add ice to a mixing glass, then add the bitters, rum, vermouth, and simple syrup. Stir at least forty times. Empty the cocktail glass, then strain the contents of the mixing glass into the empty cocktail glass. Garnish with a cherry. Serve.

Ambassador Joseph C. Wilson was the United States' top diplomat in Gabon and São Tomé and Príncipe from 1992 to 1995 during the George H. W. Bush presidency, but he is perhaps best known as the husband of CIA officer Valerie Plame. During the presidency of George W. Bush, Plame was burned by sources in the White House who leaked her identity to *Washington Post* columnist Robert Novak. No one was ever held responsible for this intelligence breach. In 2007, Plame authored a book, *Fair Game: My Life as a Spy, My Betrayal by the White House*. She now writes spy novels with Sarah Lovett. Their first book was *Blowback*, which was followed by *Burned*.

Ambassador

1 ounce rum
⅓ ounce apple schnapps
½ ounce passion fruit liqueur
1 ounce cranberry juice

Add ice and water to a cocktail glass to chill the glass. Add ice to the tin side of a Boston shaker. In the mixing glass, add the rum, apple schnapps, passion fruit liqueur, and cranberry juice. Pour the contents of the mixing glass into the iced tin and secure the glass to the tin. Shake the contents until the ice sounds different and the contents are cold. Open the Boston shaker. Empty the cocktail glass, refill with ice, and then strain the contents of the shaker into the glass. Serve.

When you are a spy, some mornings are difficult to face: a dark morning! You might be bruised physically or emotionally from the night before because of a failed mission.

Dark Morning

1 ounce rum
1 ounce coffee liqueur
½ ounce chocolate syrup
¼ ounce simple syrup
5 to 6 ounces milk

Add ice to a highball glass to chill the glass. Add ice to the tin side of a Boston shaker. In the mixing glass, add the rum,

*coffee liqueur, chocolate syrup, simple syrup, and milk. Pour
the contents of the mixing glass into the iced tin and secure
the glass to the tin. Shake the contents until the ice sounds
different and the contents are cold. Open the Boston shaker.
Strain the contents of the shaker into the ice-filled glass.
Serve.*

Sometimes spies work alone, but mostly they work as part of
a team. It is always better to be able to double-team someone
instead of working alone. Here the dark rum and the amaretto work together for a tasty shot!

Double Team

1 ounce dark rum
1 ounce amaretto

*Prepare a shot glass. Add ice to the tin side of a Boston
shaker. In the mixing glass, add the rum and amaretto. Pour
the contents of the mixing glass into the iced tin and secure
the glass to the tin. Shake the contents until the ice sounds
different and the contents are cold. Open the Boston shaker.
Strain the contents of the shaker into the shot glass. Serve.*

In 1977, Roger Moore starred as James Bond in *The Spy Who
Loved Me*. The film opens with Bond in a mountain cabin
where he has spent time with a woman. As he prepares to
leave, she says, "James, I need you," to which he replies, "So
does England."

He begins to ski down the mountain. The audience understands that James has been the victim of a honey trap when the woman radios to a contact, "He has just left. He has just left. Over and out."

Her contact, a group leader, responds, "Message received. We are waiting. Over and out," and then leads the group of four in an armed skiing pursuit of James Bond. With some fancy skiing, James is able to avoid the bullets, but then he skis off a cliff. After a moment, a Union Jack parachute appears, and the James Bond theme is cued for the audience to enjoy.

DOWNHILL RACER

2 ounces rum
2 ounces orange juice
2 ounces pineapple juice

Add ice to a highball glass to chill the glass. Add ice to the tin side of a Boston shaker. In the mixing glass, add the rum, pineapple juice, and orange juice. Pour the contents of the mixing glass into the iced tin and secure the glass to the tin. Shake the contents until the ice sounds different and the contents are cold. Open the Boston shaker. Empty the highball glass, then add ice and strain the contents of the shaker into the ice-filled glass. Serve.

A true Dark 'n' Stormy includes both Gosling's Black Seal Rum and Gosling's Stormy Ginger Beer. The Gosling brothers' company is located on the Island of Bermuda. Depending on how Dark 'n' Stormy you want your drink, the brothers Gosling sell 80-proof, 140-proof, and 151-proof rum.

Dark 'n' Stormy

1 ½ ounces Gosling's Black Seal Rum
5 ounces Gosling's Stormy Ginger Beer
Lime slice

Add ice to a highball glass. Add the rum and then the ginger beer. Stir gently. Add the lime wedge to the side of the glass for garnish. Serve.

The US Navy's special operations force is known as the SEALs, which is an acronym for sea, air, and land teams. While SEALs are members of the US Navy, they have partnered in the past with the CIA. This partnership is highlighted in the Kathryn Bigelow movie *Zero Dark Thirty*, which tells the real-life story of the CIA manhunt for Osama bin Laden. The movie starred Jessica Chastain and was nominated for five Academy Awards. Here is my version of this drink to celebrate these American heroes.

Navy SEAL

1 ounce rum
1 ounce bourbon

Prepare a large shot glass. Add ice to the tin side of a Boston shaker. In the mixing glass, add the rum and bourbon. Pour the contents of the mixing glass into the iced tin and secure the glass to the tin. Shake the contents until the ice sounds different and the contents are cold. Open the Boston shaker.

Strain the contents of the shaker into the empty shot glass. Serve.

The idea behind US intelligence operations on others is to ensure that we are able to maintain liberty. A great example of this idea is featured in the Michael Bay film *Pearl Harbor*. Dan Aykroyd plays Capt. Raymond Thurman, a naval intelligence officer who believes that a Japanese attack on American naval forces is imminent at Pearl Harbor based on the information that he gathered related to Japanese communications.

LIBERTY

1 ounce rum
1 ounce calvados
⅓ ounce lemon juice
⅔ ounce simple syrup

Add ice and water to a cocktail glass to chill the glass. Add ice to the tin side of a Boston shaker. In the mixing glass, add the rum, calvados, lemon juice, and simple syrup. Pour the contents of the mixing glass into the iced tin and secure the glass to the tin. Shake the contents until the ice sounds different and the contents are cold. Open the Boston shaker. Strain the contents of the shaker into the iced glass. Serve.

Dan Aykroyd is no stranger to playing an intelligence officer. In 1985, Aykroyd was part of a trio that wrote the screenplay for the John Landis film *Spies Like Us*. Aykroyd also starred in the movie alongside Chevy Chase, Donna Dixon, and Bruce Davison. The story follows two spies, Emmett Fitz-Hume (Chase) and Austin Millbarge (Aykroyd), through selection, training, and execution of their first mission, which takes them into the Soviet-controlled mountains, where they run into Soviet agents and a Soviet nuclear missile crew. Toward the end of the movie, with the destruction of the earth close at hand, all the agents, officers, and crew members pair up to make love, not war. Sir Paul McCartney wrote and performed the title song. McCartney also wrote and performed the title song for the James Bond film *Live and Let Die*.

LOVE IN THE AFTERNOON

2 ounces dark rum
1 ounce orange juice
1 ounce coconut cream
½ ounce strawberry liqueur
½ ounce heavy cream
6 strawberries
2 cups ice

Add ice and water to a goblet or wine glass to chill the glass. Add ice to a blender, and then add the rum, orange juice, coconut cream, strawberry liqueur, heavy cream, and five strawberries. Blend until smooth. Empty the goblet or wine glass. Pour the contents of the blender into the chilled glass. Garnish with the sixth strawberry. Serve.

In southern Nevada on the southern shore of the Groom Lake salt flat, there is a secret military base known as Area 51. Little is known other than the base exists, which leads to speculation because the area is restricted. The CIA first acknowledged the existence of the base in 2013. The correct name for the facility is Homey Airport.

Nevada

2 ounces rum
1 ounce grapefruit juice
½ ounce lime juice
¼ ounce simple syrup
Dash Angostura bitters

Add ice and water to a cocktail glass to chill the glass. Add ice to the tin side of a Boston shaker. In the mixing glass, add the rum, Angostura bitters, grapefruit juice, lime juice, and simple syrup. Pour the contents of the mixing glass into the iced tin and secure the glass to the tin. Shake the contents until the ice sounds different and the contents are cold. Open the Boston shaker. Empty the glass and strain the contents of the shaker into the empty glass. Serve.

TEQUILA AND MESCAL COCKTAILS

Tequila and mescal are both made from the agave plant. The agave plant takes between eight and twelve years to reach maturity, which means tequila makers must project the demand for tequila a decade in advance. Like rum, tequila is aged to varying degrees in burned oak barrels—many of which are used bourbon and cognac barrels. As the tequila ages, the charred barrels lend more color to the spirit. Blanco or plata is tequila that is aged less than two months in stainless-steel or neutral oak barrels. Joven or oro is generally unaged tequila that is flavored with caramel coloring. Reposado is tequila that is aged a minimum of two months but less than a year in oak barrels. Añejo is tequila that is aged for a minimum of a year but less than three years in oak barrels. Finally, extra añejo is aged for a minimum of three years in oak barrels. The longer the tequila is aged, the darker the liquid becomes and the more influence the wood has on the flavor—and the higher the price of the tequila. Cocktails rarely call for the pricy, long-aged tequilas.

I Spy was a hit series that ran for three seasons between 1965 and 1968 starring Robert Culp and Bill Cosby. The series followed US intelligence agents Kelly Robinson and Alexander Scott as they traveled the world undercover as a tennis player and his trainer. One of their stops took them to Acapulco, Mexico.

ACAPULCO

1 ½ ounces tequila
3 ounces pineapple juice
1 ounce grapefruit juice

Add ice and water to a cocktail glass to chill the glass. Add ice to the tin side of a Boston shaker. In the mixing glass, add the tequila, pineapple juice, and grapefruit juice. Pour the contents of the mixing glass into the iced tin and secure the glass to the tin. Shake the contents until the ice sounds different and the contents are cold. Open the Boston shaker.

Empty the cocktail glass and strain the contents of the shaker into the iced glass. Serve.

Jeremy Renner is a very talented actor who portrayed Aaron Cross in the blockbuster *The Bourne Legacy*. The movie opens on Cross surviving the Alaskan wilderness in the middle of winter as he moves toward a secret cabin used by agents or officers in his operation. Once there, he hopes to find some meds so he can continue to perform at a high level. *The Bourne Legacy* is part of the Bourne series of movies and the first not to feature the main character Jason Bourne, played by Matt Damon.

ALASKA WHITE

1 ounce tequila
1 ounce vodka
½ ounce gin
½ ounce sambuca
4 to 6 ounces Sprite or other lemon-lime soda

Add ice to a Collins glass to chill. Add the tequila, vodka, gin, and sambuca, and then fill with the lemon-lime soda. Serve.

A siesta is a traditional afternoon nap in Spain after lunch to beat the afternoon heat. There are many health benefits to a nap in the afternoon that might be to the spy's advantage.

SIESTA

1 ½ ounces tequila
¾ ounce lime juice
½ ounce sloe gin

Add ice and water to a cocktail glass to chill the glass. Add ice to the tin side of a Boston shaker. In the mixing glass, add the tequila, lime juice, and sloe gin. Pour the contents of the mixing glass into the iced tin and secure the glass to the tin. Shake the contents until the ice sounds different and the contents are cold. Open the Boston shaker. Strain the contents of the shaker into the iced glass. Serve.

A spy must be ready to deceive. This deception is best if the lie is based in the truth so that the spy remembers and is less likely to be caught.

DECEIVER

2 ounces tequila
1 ounce Galliano

Add ice and water to a cocktail glass to chill the glass. Add ice to the tin side of a Boston shaker. In the mixing glass, add the tequila and Galliano. Pour the contents of the mixing glass into the iced tin and secure the glass to the tin. Shake the contents until the ice sounds different and the contents are cold. Open the Boston shaker. Strain the contents of the shaker into the iced glass. Serve.

A flat tire or other car trouble is usually not a good development, but for a spy it may just be a cover. Adolf Eichmann was a lieutenant colonel in the German SS and was tasked with deporting and exterminating Jews during World War II. After the war, Eichmann was helped by Bishop Alois Hudal, who organized the "ratline" for many Nazi soldiers to move from Europe to South America. Eichmann changed his name to Ricardo Klement and moved to Argentina. This was where a Mossad team found him in 1960. The Israeli intelligence agency had worked on this case for many years. The team entered Argentina without weapons and kidnapped the former SS officer after pretending to have car trouble. They moved Eichmann to a safe house and waited to sneak him out of Argentina and to Israel, where Eichmann stood trial and was executed for his crimes. In 2018, the film *Operation Finale*, detailing the Mossad action, was released; it starred Oscar Isaac as Mossad agent Peter Malkin, Lior Raz as Mossad director Isser Harel, and Ben Kingsley as Adolf Eichmann.

Flat Tire

1 ounce tequila
½ ounce black sambuca

Pour the tequila and black sambuca into the shot glass. Serve.

In 2018 the action comedy *The Spy Who Dumped Me*, starring Mila Kunis and Kate McKinnon, was released. The story follows two friends as they find out that a former boyfriend of one of them is a CIA agent. The two friends are sucked into the world of espionage. This cocktail is a new version of the Vieux Carré.

NOUVEAU CARRÉ

1 ½ ounces añejo tequila
¾ ounce Bénédictine
¼ ounce Lillet Blanc
5 dashes Peychaud's Bitters
Lemon twist

Add ice to an old-fashioned glass to chill the glass. Add the bitters, Lillet Blanc, Bénédictine, and tequila. Stir. Add ice and garnish with a lemon twist. Serve.

Pineapple and coconut, yum! The combination of the two tropical flavors are refreshing. The addition of tequila only amplifies the flavor combination.

TEQUILA COLADA VERSUS PIÑA COLADA

2 ounces tequila
1 ½ ounces coconut cream
2 ounces pineapple juice
Pineapple spear

Add ice and water to a hurricane glass to chill the glass. Add ice to the tin side of a Boston shaker. In the mixing glass, add the tequila, coconut cream, and pineapple juice. Pour the contents of the mixing glass into the iced tin and secure the glass to the tin. Shake the contents until the ice sounds different and the contents are cold. Open the Boston shaker. Empty the hurricane glass, then fill with ice. Strain the contents of the shaker into the glass. Garnish with the pineapple spear. Serve.

Note: This drink can also be blended with one cup of ice. For a piña colada, replace the tequila with rum.

Silk stockings are elegant and something that any spy might desire. However, beware that silk stockings might be a tip-off about a honey trap in the making or an elegant gift from a raven to seduce a lady with information.

SILK STOCKING

1 ½ ounces tequila
½ ounce crème de cacao (dark)
½ ounce raspberry liqueur
1 ounce cream

Add ice and water to a cocktail glass to chill the glass. Add ice to the tin side of a Boston shaker. In the mixing glass, add the tequila, crème de cacao, raspberry liqueur, and cream. Pour the contents of the mixing glass into the iced tin and secure the glass to the tin. Shake the contents until the ice sounds different and the contents are cold. Open the Boston shaker. Empty the glass. Strain the contents of the shaker into the iced glass. Serve.

Every night leads to a sunrise. If a spy is going to start the morning with a drink, consider the Tequila Sunrise.

Tequila Sunrise

1 ½ ounces tequila
3 ounces orange juice
½ ounce grenadine syrup
Orange slice
Cocktail cherry

Add ice to an old-fashioned glass to chill the glass. Add tequila and orange juice. Add the grenadine, which will sink to the bottom of the glass, then stir gently. Garnish with orange slice and cocktail cherry. Serve.

Every sunrise leads to a sunset. A spy might consider ending their day with a Tequila Sunset.

Tequila Sunset

1 ½ ounces tequila
½ ounce orange juice
½ ounce lemon juice
¼ ounce Chambord
¾ ounce honey

*Add ice and water to a cocktail glass to chill the glass. Add
ice to the tin side of a Boston shaker. In the mixing glass, add
the tequila, orange juice, and lemon juice. Pour the contents
of the mixing glass into the iced tin and secure the glass to
the tin. Shake the contents until the ice sounds different
and the contents are cold. Open the Boston shaker. Empty
the glass and pour the honey into the inside rim of the glass.
Strain the contents of the shaker into the iced glass. Pour the
Chambord on top. Serve.*

Tequila in a mule cocktail is a wonderful addition to this classic drink. A spy might request this riff on this cocktail for a
twist. For a Moscow Mule, substitute vodka for the tequila
in this cocktail.

MAYAN MULE VERSUS THE MOSCOW MULE

1 ounce lime juice
(reserve one half of the lime for garnish)
½ ounce simple syrup
1 ½ ounces tequila or mescal
4 ounces ginger beer

*Add ice to an old-fashioned glass or a copper mug to chill
the glass. Add the lime juice, simple syrup, and tequila. Stir
to mix the three ingredients. Add the ginger beer and stir
gently. Garnish with lime peel. Serve.*

Every spy has enjoyed a margarita at one time or another. Who hasn't? It is a wonderful drink that balances sweet and sour. Any cocktail book is incomplete without one.

Margarita

1 ½ ounces tequila
¾ ounce Cointreau
¾ ounce lime juice
Lime wedge
Lime slice
Kosher salt for the rim

Add ice and water to a margarita glass to chill the glass. Set up a plate of kosher salt. Add ice to the tin side of a Boston shaker. In the mixing glass, add the tequila, Cointreau, and lime juice. Pour the contents of the mixing glass into the iced tin and secure the glass to the tin. Shake the contents until the ice sounds different and the contents are cold. Open the Boston shaker. Empty the cocktail glass. Take the lime wedge and wipe the outside of the glass. Gently place the side rim of the glass into the salt; then strain the contents of the shaker into the empty glass. Garnish with a lime. Serve.

A traditional sangrita is served with a shot of tequila as a chaser for the spirit. The following is a traditional recipe for sangrita, which does not have tomato, a secret that a spy would know.

Sangrita

1 ½ ounces tequila
1 ounce orange juice
¾ ounce lime juice
½ ounce pomegranate juice
3 dashes Tabasco sauce
1 slice jalapeño

Pour the tequila in a shot glass. In a small bowl, mix orange juice, lime juice, pomegranate juice, and Tabasco sauce. Pour the mixture into another shot glass. Garnish with a slice of jalapeño. Serve.

BRANDY COCKTAILS

Brandy is distilled wine. Most brandy has a golden hue from barrel aging; however, some brandy is clear. That occurs when the barrels are old and used, with no color left to lend to the brandy, or the brandy may not have been aged at all. Cognac, Armagnac, and calvados are three examples of famous French brandy. Cognac is distilled from a wine made from a mixture of mostly ugni blanc (Trebbiano) and, to a lesser extent, folle blanche and Colombard. Cognac comes from the Cognac region just north of Bordeaux. Armagnac starts as grape wine from ten different grapes but consists mostly of the same grapes used to make cognac. Armagnac is produced in the Armagnac region in Gascony in South West France. Calvados begins as apple wine in the northern Normandy region of France.

The longer brandy is aged, the higher the price. For cocktails, you may consider using younger product unless you are trying to make a statement—but know that the subtle differences that are clear to the palate are lost in the mixture of a cocktail. Brandy is made in the Americas also, with examples from both North and South America. Cognac, Armagnac, and calvados are all considered luxury products, which is why they would be the product of choice of the spy, such as James Bond, with a seemingly unlimited expense account. For those secret agents on limited expense accounts, there are excellent substitutes at lower price points.

Secret agents know how to block punches and fall down stairs, both of which are occupational hazards. Legend has the Block and Fall cocktail created in the coastal town of Deauville in northern France in 1924. The stylish town is known for horse breeding, a film festival, and luxury hotels that feature casinos. Many people believe that Ian Fleming took locational inspiration for his first book, *Casino Royale*, from the town of Deauville. Please note the French influence of the drink in all four components in the cocktail.

BLOCK AND FALL

1 ounce cognac
1 ounce Cointreau
½ ounce absinthe
½ ounces calvados

Add ice and water to a cocktail glass to chill the glass. Add ice to the tin side of a Boston shaker. In the mixing glass, add the cognac, Cointreau, absinthe, and calvados. Pour the contents of the mixing glass into the iced tin and secure the glass to the tin. Shake the contents until the ice sounds different

and the contents are cold. Open the Boston shaker. Empty
the cocktail glass, then strain the contents of the shaker into
the empty glass. Serve.

Even though in the movies James Bond is usually seen driving an Aston Martin, an Audi, an Alfa Romeo, a BMW, or a Jaguar, in the novels, Ian Fleming featured luxury cars from Bentley as the cars of choice of the world's favorite secret agent. In *Casino Royale*, *Live and Let Die*, and *Moonraker*, Bond drives a 1930s-era Bentley 4 ½ Litre. Bentley cars are featured in Fleming's *Thunderball* and a continuation of the Bond series by John Gardner in the 1984 release *Role of Honour*.

BENTLEY

1 ½ ounces sweet vermouth
1 ½ ounces calvados
Orange twist

Add ice and water to a cocktail glass to chill the glass. Add
ice to a mixing glass, then add the vermouth and calvados.
Stir forty times. Empty the cocktail glass, then strain the
contents of the mixing glass into the empty glass. Garnish
with an orange twist. Serve.

Just when we think there is no escape for our hero—the hero is able to evade the jaws of death! Secret agents seem to have nine lives, eluding death with the grace and nimbleness of a cat. Perhaps the agent or officer imbibes in a Corpse Reviver.

All sources agree that this cocktail was created at the Savoy Hotel in London.

CORPSE REVIVER #3
(THE SAVOY CORPSE REVIVER)

1 ounce brandy
1 ounce Fernet-Branca
1 ounce white crème de menthe

Add ice and water to a cocktail glass to chill the glass. Add ice to a mixing glass, then add the brandy, Fernet-Branca, and white crème de menthe. Stir forty times. Empty the cocktail glass, then strain the contents of the mixing glass into the empty glass. Serve.

The CIA and MI6 are both charged with helping their governments deal with foreign affairs and with not allowing relations between countries to get out of hand. The movie *The Sum of All Fears*, based on the Tom Clancy novel of the same name, is a good example. In the movie, a young Jack Ryan, played by Ben Affleck, helps the United States avoid nuclear war by exercising a back channel with Russian Federation president Alexander Nemerov when US president J. Robert Fowler, thinking that the Russians are behind a nuclear bomb detonation in Baltimore harbor, considers a retaliatory nuclear strike. The movie has similar plot points as the novel but deviates in some key aspects for a completely different story.

Foreign Affair

1 ounce brandy
1 ounce black sambuca

Pour both of the ingredients into a brandy snifter. Swirl the snifter to mix the two spirits together. Serve.

Shanghai's Century Park has a statue commemorating Li Bai, a famous spy for the Chinese Communist Party, on the site of his execution. During the Japanese occupation of China during World War II, Li Bai established a secret radio station in Shanghai. He was arrested several times for his operation, first by the Japanese and later by the Nationalist Party of China (Kuomintang of China—KMT). After World War II, Li Bai worked for the KMT but spied for the Communist Party. He sent KMT information to the Chinese Communist Party, which sealed his fate. Generalissimo Chiang Kai-shek signed a writ of execution, and Li Bai was executed in 1949 before he reached the age of forty.

Shanghai

1 ounce brandy
½ ounce Curaçao
¼ ounce maraschino liqueur
2 dashes Angostura bitters
Lemon zest spiral
Cocktail cherry

Add ice and water to a cocktail glass to chill the glass. Add ice to the tin side of a Boston shaker. In the mixing glass, add the Angostura bitters, brandy, Curaçao, and maraschino liqueur. Pour the contents of the mixing glass into the iced tin and secure the glass to the tin. Shake the contents until the ice sounds different and the contents are cold. Open the Boston shaker. Empty the cocktail glass, then strain the contents of the shaker into the empty glass. Garnish with a lemon zest spiral and a cocktail cherry. Serve.

Charles Henry Maxwell Knight, OBE, was a British spymaster and part of the inspiration for M in the James Bond series. Knight served as a British navy officer during World War I and, after that period, in MI5. Knight was a noted naturalist and author of more than thirty-four texts. He was also a broadcaster on the BBC, hosting nature-themed shows. He juggled his MI5 duties at the same time he was the public face of BBC nature shows.

KNIGHT

2 ounces brandy
½ ounce lemon juice
¼ ounce Cointreau
¼ ounce Chartreuse
¼ ounce half-and-half

Add ice and water to a cocktail glass to chill the glass. Add ice to the tin side of a Boston shaker. In the mixing glass, add the brandy, lemon juice, Cointreau, Chartreuse, and half-and-half. Pour the contents of the mixing glass into the iced tin and secure the glass to the tin. Shake the contents until the ice sounds different and the contents are cold. Open the Boston shaker. Empty the cocktail glass, then strain the contents of the shaker into the empty glass. Serve.

Sir Sean Connery and Sir Roger Moore, both of whom played James Bond, have something in common with most of the former chiefs of the Secret Intelligence Services (MI6). They were all knighted by the British monarch. Connery is a Knight Bachelor and Moore a Knight Commander of the Most Excellent Order of the British Empire (KBE), while most of the chiefs of MI6 are Knight Commanders of the Most Distinguished Order of Saint Michael and Saint George (KCMG). James Bond is honored with Companion of the Order of St. Michael and St. George (CMG) in *From Russia with Love* but turns down KCMG in the novel *The Man with the Golden Gun*. American Jack Ryan is honored with Knight Commander of the Royal Victorian Order (KCVO) in the novel and movie *Patriot Games*. This cocktail celebrates all knights.

SIR KNIGHT

2 ounces cognac
½ ounce Cointreau
½ ounce Chartreuse
Dash Angostura bitters

Add ice and water to a cocktail glass to chill the glass. Add ice to the tin side of a Boston shaker. In the mixing glass, add the Angostura bitters, Chartreuse, Cointreau, and cognac. Pour the contents of the mixing glass into the iced tin and

*secure the glass to the tin. Shake the contents until the ice
sounds different and the contents are cold. Open the Boston
shaker. Empty the cocktail glass, then strain the contents of
the shaker into the empty glass. Serve.*

Spying can either help or hurt international relations. That is
part of the reason for the United Nations. This organization
gives every country a forum to speak to each other and to
help take care of each other before an international incident.

INTERNATIONAL COCKTAIL

1 ½ ounces cognac
1 ounce triple sec
1 ounce anisette
½ ounce vodka

*Add ice and water to a cocktail glass to chill the glass. Add
ice to the tin side of a Boston shaker. In the mixing glass, add
vodka, anisette, triple sec, and cognac. Pour the contents of
the mixing glass into the iced tin and secure the glass to the
tin. Shake the contents until the ice sounds different and
the contents are cold. Open the Boston shaker. Empty the
cocktail glass, then strain the contents of the shaker into the
empty glass. Serve.*

According to David Embury, the Jack Rose—as well as the
sidecar—is one of the six cocktails that everyone should

know how to make. The first letter of the two names match up with those of Tom Clancy's main hero, Jack Ryan—perhaps this is code!

JACK ROSE

2 ounces apple brandy
½ ounce fresh lemon juice
¼ ounce grenadine
Superfine sugar

Set up the cocktail glasses ahead of time. Dip the edge of the cocktail glass in water, then dip in a plate of superfine sugar for a thin, even coating on the edge of the glass. Then freeze the glassware for at least thirty minutes; this can be set up the day before serving. When the glass is prepared, add ice to the tin side of a Boston shaker. In the mixing glass, add the apple brandy, lemon juice, and grenadine. Pour the contents of the mixing glass into the iced tin and secure the glass to the tin. Shake the contents until the ice sounds different and the contents are cold. Open the Boston shaker. Strain the contents of the shaker into the empty glass. Serve.

Ian Fleming introduces a terrifying form of torture to the reader when Le Chiffre tries to extract information from James Bond in *Casino Royale*. Daniel Craig (playing Bond) and Mads Mikkelsen (playing Le Chiffre) do a wonderful job bringing the literature to life in the 2006 big-screen version by the same name.

Kick in the Pants

1 ounce cognac
1 ounce bourbon
1 ounce triple sec

Add ice and water to a cocktail glass to chill the glass. Add ice to the tin side of a Boston shaker. In the mixing glass, add the cognac, bourbon, and triple sec. Pour the contents of the mixing glass into the iced tin and secure the glass to the tin. Shake the contents until the ice sounds different and the contents are cold. Open the Boston shaker. Empty the cocktail glass, then strain the contents of the shaker into the empty glass. Serve.

The Penny Marshall film *Jumpin' Jack Flash* hit the big screen in 1986 with a star-studded cast that included Whoopi Goldberg, John Wood, Stephen Collins, Jim Belushi, Annie Potts, Jeroen Krabbé, Carol Kane, Jon Lovitz, Phil Hartman, Tracey Ullman, and Gary Marshall and featured the voice and a short appearance by Jonathan Pryce. The storyline follows a computer worker at a bank, Terry (Goldberg), as she transfers funds as part of her daily routine. She intercepts a message from a British spy, codename Jumpin' Jack Flash, that starts a series of events that lead Terry down the path of espionage. The song "Jumpin' Jack Flash," by the Rolling Stones, is central to the movie.

Jumpin' Jack Flash

1 ounce brandy
1 ounce blackberry liqueur
1 ounce orange juice
¼ ounce simple syrup

Add ice and water to an old-fashioned glass to chill the glass. Add ice to the tin side of a Boston shaker. In the mixing glass, add the simple syrup, orange juice, blackberry liqueur, and brandy. Pour the contents of the mixing glass into the iced tin and secure the glass to the tin. Shake the contents until the ice sounds different and the contents are cold. Open the Boston shaker. Strain the contents of the shaker into the ice-filled old-fashioned glass. Serve.

Trinitrotoluene, better known as TNT, is an explosive chemical compound. TNT can be of great use to a spy to enter or exit an area or just to cause confusion.

TNT

2 ounces brandy
1 ounce triple sec
¼ ounce pastis

Add ice and water to a cocktail glass to chill the glass. Add ice to the tin side of a Boston shaker. In the mixing glass, add the brandy, triple sec, and pastis. Pour the contents of the mixing glass into the iced tin and secure the glass to the tin. Shake the contents until the ice sounds different and the contents are cold. Open the Boston shaker. Empty the cocktail glass, then strain the contents of the shaker into the empty glass. Serve.

==

WHISKEY COCKTAILS

Whiskey (or whisky outside of the US) is the largest differentiated spirit category. This spirit is traditionally made in Scotland, Ireland, Canada, and the United States. Whiskey is distilled from beer made from grain. Each tradition uses different grain or a grain mixture for the distiller's beer. The beer is then distilled into a clear spirit and aged in oak barrels for a short or extended period. The longer the whiskey is aged, the higher the price of the spirit. Most Scotch whisky is made from malt and grain whiskies and aged in a variety of used barrels, including bourbon, sherry, and porto barrels. Scotch has a unique smoked, peaty flavor and aroma. Most Scotch is aged for at least four years, but it can be aged for much, much longer. Irish whiskey has a light, mild flavor and aroma and can be made from a variety of grains. This spirit is aged for at least three years, but much is aged longer. Canadian whisky is mild flavored, made from multiple grains, and is aged for at least three years. Bourbon is one of the most highly regulated whiskies made in the United States (of which 95 percent is made in Kentucky). It is made from at least 51 percent corn (most bourbon distillers use more—closer to 65–75 percent). As bourbon comes off the still, it must be less than 160 proof. Only water can be added to bourbon; as bourbon is added to newly charred oak barrels, the proof must fall between 80 and 125. There is no minimum age for bourbon, but if it is aged less than two years, an age statement must appear on the label. Most bourbon is aged for at least four years. Other whiskies are usually defined by the grain from which they are primary made. For example, corn whiskey is at least 80 percent corn, rye whiskey is at least 51 percent rye, and wheat whiskey is at least 51 percent wheat.

War has always been fought by an agreed upon set of rules—"gentleman's rules." In 1940, British prime minister Winston Churchill helped organize the Special Operations Executive (SOE). They were known informally as the Ministry of Ungentlemanly Warfare, the Baker Street Irregulars, and Churchill's Secret Army—needless to say, they did not always follow the rules. The SOE did not limit membership—in fact more than one-quarter of the forces were female. The SOE's mission was to conduct espionage, sabotage, and reconnaissance on the European continent. SOE also operated in Southeast Asia, and plans were in place for a British group that would resist on the British Isle if a German invasion was successful. In 2018, Netflix Original produced a series called *Churchill's Secret Agents: The New Recruits*. The series has five episodes and follows a group of prospective officers through selection, training, survival skills, and finishing school (which includes cryptography training and a final exam). Not all of the cast members who start the show finish; in fact, four are eliminated in the first episode. The actual SOE was disbanded in 1946. This cocktail celebrates Churchill.

CHURCHILL

1 ½ ounces Scotch whisky
½ ounce sweet vermouth
½ ounce Cointreau
½ ounce Lime juice

Add ice and water to a cocktail glass to chill the glass. Add ice to the tin side of the shaker. Pour the whisky, vermouth, Cointreau, and lime juice into the mixing glass side and attach the two sides together. Shake until you hear the sound of the ice change. Empty the cocktail glass, then strain the contents of the shaker into the empty cocktail glass. Serve.

James Bond has been approached in several novels and movies by a nerida. From Greek, *nerida* means "sea nymph or mermaid." Ian Fleming created the character Honeychile Rider for the novel *Dr. No*, and she very much fits the nerida persona; we read that she supports herself as a shell diver. Her name was shortened for the movie to Honey Ryder, where she was played by Ursula Andress. Ryder wakes a beach-sleeping Bond (Sean Connery) by singing as she emerges from the ocean. Bond pulls his gun and looks to the edge of the beach, where Ryder is walking out of the surf. Sensing no danger, Bond holsters his gun and sings back to Ryder, who is startled.

Ryder asks Bond, "What are you doing here? Looking for shells?"

Bond responds, "No . . . I'm just looking."

NERIDA

3 ounces Scotch whisky
½ ounce lime juice or lemon juice
6 ounces dry ginger ale
Lime wheel or lemon wheel

Add ice and water to a Collins glass to chill the glass. Add ice to the tin side of a Boston shaker. In the mixing glass, add the Scotch and lime juice (or lemon juice). Pour the contents of the mixing glass into the iced tin and secure the glass to the tin. Shake the contents until the ice sounds different and the contents are cold. Open the Boston shaker. Empty the Collins glass, fill with ice, and then strain the contents of the shaker into the ice-filled glass. Then fill the glass with ginger ale, gently stirring the mixture. Garnish with the lime (or lemon) wheel. Serve.

The original cocktail was created at the beginning of the Revolutionary War in the town of Elmsford, New York, perhaps by Betsy Flanagan. According to legend, Flanagan decorated the glasses with a feather from the tail of a rooster; the name *cocktail* was born. General George Washington founded the Culper Ring, led by Maj. Benjamin Tallmadge. The first American spies were able to uncover many British plots, including Maj. Gen. Benedict Arnold and British Maj. John Andre conspiring to surrender the fort at West Point. Surely, many of the original American spies enjoyed the original cocktail.

THE OLD-FASHIONED

¼ ounce simple syrup
2 or 3 dashes of Angostura bitters
2 ounces bourbon
Orange slice
Cocktail cherry

Pour the simple syrup into the bottom of an old-fashioned glass, followed by the bitters and then the bourbon. Add ice to the glass and stir. Garnish with an orange slice and a cocktail cherry. Serve.

Ian Fleming's seventh James Bond novel is *Goldfinger*. Bond tracks and foils an attempt by Auric Goldfinger on the US gold reserve at Fort Knox, Kentucky. In the movie adaptation by the same name, Goldfinger offers Bond, played by Sean Connery, a mint julep as they discuss "operation grand slam." During the conversation, Bond figures out that Goldfinger plans to nuke the gold supply at Fort Knox.

Mint Julep

¼ ounce simple syrup
4 to 6 mint leaves
2 to 3 ounces bourbon
Mint sprig

Add the simple syrup to a pewter or silver julep cup. Lay the leaves out on your palm and lightly smack them with your other hand. Add them to the cup. Add the bourbon and mix. Then add crushed ice. Smack the mint sprig between your hands and add to the julep. Serve.

James Armistead was an enslaved man from Virginia who asked his owner, William Armistead, if he could volunteer to fight for the Revolutionary cause. He served under Maj. Gen. Gilbert du Motier, better known as the Marquis de Lafayette. Lafayette used him as a spy—and he became a double agent. The information delivered helped the Americans defeat the British at Yorktown. James Armistead adopted the French nobleman's title as his last name once he was freed by the Virginia Assembly in 1787.

Lafayette

2 ounces bourbon
½ ounce Dubonnet
½ ounce dry vermouth
1 dash Angostura bitters
Cocktail cherry

Add ice and water to a cocktail glass to chill the glass. Add ice in a mixing glass. Then add the bitters, bourbon, Dubonnet, and dry vermouth and stir at least forty times. Empty the cocktail glass and strain the contents of the mixing glass into the cocktail glass. Garnish with a cocktail cherry and serve.

Note: You can also serve the Lafayette in an old-fashioned glass over ice.

The title Kentucky Colonel is an honor awarded by the governor of the Commonwealth of Kentucky to deserving people inside and outside the commonwealth. President George H. W. Bush was a Kentucky Colonel. He was also the US director of Central Intelligence and the only former president to have held that office.

Kentucky Colonel

1 ½ ounces bourbon
½ ounce Bénédictine
Lemon twist

Add ice and water to a cocktail glass to chill the glass. Add ice to the tin side of a Boston shaker. Add bourbon and Bénédictine to the mixing glass. Pour the contents of the mixing glass into the iced tin and secure the glass to the tin. Shake the contents until the ice sounds different and the contents are cold. Open the Boston shaker. Empty the cocktail glass, then strain the contents of the shaker into the empty glass. Garnish with the lemon twist. Serve.

Spies who like cosmopolitans might try this twist on a cosmo or substitute vodka for the bourbon for the traditional drink.

Kentucky Cosmo

1 ½ ounces bourbon
½ ounce Cointreau
½ ounce lime juice
1 ounce cranberry juice
Orange twist

Add ice and water to a cocktail glass to chill the glass. Add ice to the tin side of a Boston shaker. Add bourbon, Cointreau, lime juice, and cranberry juice to the mixing glass. Pour the contents of the mixing glass into the iced tin and secure the glass to the tin. Shake the contents until the ice sounds different and the contents are cold. Open the Boston shaker. Empty the cocktail glass, then strain the contents of the shaker into the empty glass. Garnish with an orange twist. Serve.

Pussy Galore is featured in both the novel and movie *Gold-finger* and is based on Ian Fleming's mistress, Blanche Black-well. Actress Honor Blackman portrayed Galore on the silver screen.

PUSSYCAT

1 ½ ounces bourbon
1 ounce lime juice
2 ounces orange juice
¼ ounce grenadine
½ ounce simple syrup
Cocktail cherry

Add ice to an old-fashioned glass. Add ice to the tin side of a Boston shaker. In the mixing glass, add the bourbon, lime juice, orange juice, grenadine, and simple syrup. Pour the contents of the mixing glass into the iced tin and secure the glass to the tin. Shake the contents until the ice sounds different and the contents are cold. Open the Boston shaker. Strain the contents of the shaker into the old-fashioned glass. Garnish with a cocktail cherry and serve.

Roger Moore starred in *Live and Let Die*, which was filmed in Louisiana. The Sazerac, "the official cocktail of New Orleans," competes with the old-fashioned as the original cocktail. If the stories are true, the cocktail is a Spanish or French invention, not an American one, as Spain controlled New Orleans from 1763 to 1802 and France from 1718 to 1763 and from 1802 to 1803. The original Sazerac featured cognac, but the phylloxera plague made it necessary to substitute rye.

Sazerac

⅓ ounce absinthe
¼ ounce simple syrup
2 dashes Peychaud's Bitters
2 ounces rye whiskey (or cognac)
Lemon peel

Add ice and water to an old-fashioned glass to chill the glass. Once the glass is chilled, add the absinthe and swirl to cover sides of the glass. Discard the excess absinthe—whatever doesn't adhere to the glass. Add the simple syrup to the bottom of the glass, followed by the bitters. Add the rye to the glass and then ice. Stir. Twist the lemon twist above the drink and wipe it on the rim of the glass. Serve the lemon twist with the drink. Serve.

The mai tai is a classic cocktail created in 1944 by Victor "Trader Vic" Bergeron. Here is a twist on this classic drink that will please any spy.

BLUEGRASS MAI TAI

2 ounces bourbon
½ ounce Cointreau
1 ounce lemon juice
½ ounce orgeat syrup

Add ice to an old-fashioned glass to chill the glass. Add ice to the tin side of a Boston shaker. Add bourbon, Cointreau, lemon juice, and orgeat syrup to the mixing glass side of a Boston shaker. Pour the liquid into the tin side and close the shaker. Shake until the cocktail is cold. Strain the cocktail into the old-fashioned glass. Serve.

Ethan Hunt is a member of the Impossible Missions Force (IMF), played by Tom Cruise on the big screen. Six films have been produced so far in the twenty-two-year run of this incarnation of the franchise. In the second film, *Mission: Impossible 2*, Hunt has a race against time to prevent a global pandemic of a genetically modified virus called Chimera. Near the climax of the film, Hunt fights with his nemesis, Sean Ambrose, on a sandy beach.

BLOOD AND SAND

1 ounce of orange juice
1 ounce sweet vermouth
1 ounce cherry-flavored liqueur
1 ounce of blended Scotch whisky
Cocktail cherry

Add ice and water to a cocktail glass to chill the glass. Add ice to a cocktail shaker. Then add the orange juice, sweet vermouth, cherry-flavored liqueur, and blended Scotch whisky. Close the shaker and shake until the ice sounds different and the contents are cold. Empty the ice from the cocktail glass, then strain the cocktail into the glass. Garnish with a cocktail cherry and serve.

Secrets—keeping them or discovering them—are at the root of a spy's job. Depending on the need to know, a spy may have different levels of clearance, including top secret.

SECRET

1 ½ ounces Scotch
Splash white crème de menthe
6 ounces club soda

Fill a Collins glass with ice. Pour the Scotch and crème de menthe into the glass, followed by the club soda. Stir and serve.

OTHER COCKTAILS

Modern alcoholic concoctions are made from an endless combination of alcoholic beverages from many categories, including beer, wine, spirits, and liqueurs. Beer and wine are both fermented beverages. Beer is made by boiling grains to extract the sugars for fermenting to an average of 5 percent alcohol by volume. Wine is usually made from grapes. The grapes are pressed to extract the juice, which is then fermented. Wine varies in alcohol volume from 5 percent to 15 percent, with fortified wine being even higher. Fortified wine is wine with added brandy. Liqueurs are flavored, sweetened alcoholic beverages that are featured in many cocktails and serve as stand-alone after-dinner drinks, also known as cordials. The alcohol-by-volume range for most liqueurs is from 17 percent (34 proof) to 30 percent (60 proof) but can be higher than 50 percent (100 proof).

Perhaps the most important part of espionage is the ability to operate incognito. Perhaps no one knows this better than Martha "Marti" Peterson, who served as an operations officer for the CIA from 1975 to 2003. After the death of her husband, CIA officer and Green Beret John Peterson, in the Vietnam War, she volunteered to work for the CIA. In the late 1970s, Peterson was the first female agent to serve in the Moscow Bureau of the CIA. During this time, she was the handler for Alexander Ogorodnik, who was better known by his codename: Trigon. Trigon was a very important spy, as he passed a lot of sensitive information to the United States. Peterson would provide dead drops to Trigon until both were caught and taken to the infamous Lubyanka Prison. Peterson was released and returned to the United States. She would eventually remarry and have children. In retirement she authored a book about her experiences, *The Widow Spy*.

INCOGNITO

1 ½ ounces vodka
1 ounce apricot brandy
4 ounces ginger beer

Add ice to a Collins glass to chill the glass. Add the vodka, brandy, and ginger beer to the glass. Gently stir and serve.

Another incognito cocktail . . .

Incognito

2 ounces Lillet
1 ounce brandy
⅓ ounce apricot brandy
Dash Angostura bitters

Add ice and water to a cocktail glass to chill the glass. Add ice to a mixing glass, then add the Angostura bitters, Lillet, brandy, and apricot brandy. Stir forty times. Empty the ice and water out of the glass and then strain the cocktail into the glass. Serve.

Not to be confused with Ian Fleming's first novel, *Casino Royale*, and the Vesper, which Fleming features in the text, the Martini Royale is a combination between a martini and a Kir Royale. The Kir Royale is a cocktail derived from the Kir, which consists of crème de cassis and white wine. A Kir Royale is simply crème de cassis and champagne. The Martini Royale merges the martini and the Kir Royale.

Martini Royale

2 ½ ounces vodka
¼ ounce crème de cassis
2 ounces champagne
Lemon twist

Fill a cocktail glass with ice and water to chill the glass. Fill the tin side of a Boston shaker with ice. Add the vodka and crème de cassis into the glass side of the shaker, then pour the liquid into the tin and attach the two sides. Shake until the combination is cold. Discard the ice and water in the cocktail glass. Strain the mixture into the cocktail glass, top with champagne, and garnish with a lemon twist. Serve.

There are few things in this world as elegant as champagne. When life could be short or dangerous, why not indulge in something elegant?

Champagne Cocktail

7 dashes Angostura bitters
1 sugar cube
1 ounce cognac
4 to 5 ounces chilled champagne
Lemon twist
Orange twist

Prepare a champagne flute. Place a sugar cube on the end of a barspoon. Add the dashes of Angostura bitters to the sugar cube. Place the bitters-soaked sugar cube into the flute. Add the Cognac, then fill slowly with champagne, taking care not to overflow the glass. This process may take two or three slow pours. Garnish with lemon and orange twists. Serve.

People with information need to beware of the honeypot, or honey trap. There are many examples of people falling for the affections of someone they have grown close to in the lonely job of spying. The Enchantress cocktail refortifies port wine with brandy and balances the two with a little lemon juice and orange liqueur.

ENCHANTRESS

2 ounces ruby port
1 ½ ounces cognac
½ ounce Cointreau
½ ounce lemon juice
Lemon twist

Fill a cocktail glass with ice and water to chill the glass. Fill the tin side of a Boston shaker with ice. Add the port, cognac, Cointreau, and lemon juice into the glass side of the shaker, then pour the liquid into the tin and attach the two sides. Shake until the combination is cold. Discard the ice and water in the cocktail glass. Strain the Enchantress into the cocktail glass, then garnish with a lemon twist. Serve.

Alexander Litvinenko was a Russian FSB secret service agent before defecting to Great Britain. He was the author of two books, *Blowing Up Russia: Terror from Within* and *Lubyanka Criminal Group.* In 2006, he was hospitalized after becoming suddenly ill. He died twenty-three days later of radioactive poisoning from polonium-210. An extensive investigation pointed to Andrey Lugovoy as the prime suspect, in part because he met with Litvinenko the morning before he became ill. Russia refused to extradite Lugovoy, who now serves as a member of the State Duma, or the Russian Parliament. Litvinenko was only forty-three years old when he died. The Alexander is a dessert drink and should be consumed after a meal.

ALEXANDER

2 ounces gin
½ ounce cream
½ ounce crème de cacao
Lemon twist

Add ice and water to a cocktail glass to chill the glass. Add ice to the tin side of a Boston shaker. In the mixing glass, add the gin, cream, and crème de cacao. Pour the contents of the mixing glass into the iced tin and secure the glass to the tin. Shake the contents until the ice sounds different and the contents are cold. Open the Boston shaker. Empty the cocktail glass, then strain the contents of the shaker into the empty glass. Garnish with a lemon twist and serve.

The Hunt for Red October was Tom Clancy's first published novel—although he was working on several novels at once. A movie adaptation by the same name starred Alec Baldwin as Jack Ryan, Sir Sean Connery, Scott Glenn, James Earl Jones, and Sam Neill. Even though the October Revolution usually refers to the 1917 revolution and the overthrow of the Russian czar, the drink seems appropriate for Tom Clancy's "October Revolution." The book started a revolution, with many books and movies to follow.

OCTOBER REVOLUTION

1 ounce vodka
1 ounce coffee liqueur
1 ounce crème de cacao
1 ounce heavy cream

Add ice into a Collins glass. Add ice into a shaker and then add the vodka, coffee liqueur, crème de cacao, and heavy cream. Close the shaker and shake until cold. Strain the drink into the Collins glass. Serve.

Adm. John Henry Godfrey is one of the inspirations for Ian Fleming's M in the James Bond series. Godfrey served as the director of British Naval Intelligence from 1939 to 1942, during which time he held the rank of rear admiral. Ian Fleming reported directly to Godfrey. He was promoted to commander in chief of the Royal Indian Navy, a post from which he would retire in 1946 at the rank of admiral. Actor Samuel West placed Godfrey in the miniseries *Fleming: The Man Who*

Would be Bond. Godfrey would outlive Fleming, passing away in August 1970 at the age of eighty-two.

GODFREY

2 ounces cognac
½ ounce Grand Marnier
½ ounce crème de mûre
4 blackberries
Sprig of mint

Add ice and water to a cocktail glass to chill the glass. Add ice to the tin side of a Boston shaker. In the mixing glass, add the cognac, Grand Marnier, crème de mûre, and three blackberries. Pour the contents of the mixing glass into the iced tin and secure the glass to the tin. Shake the contents until the ice sounds different and the contents are cold. Open the Boston shaker. Strain the contents of the shaker into the iced glass. Garnish with a blackberry and a sprig of mint. Serve.

James Bond is the creation of author Ian Fleming. In the ten years between 1953 to 1964, Fleming established Bond as a permanent figure in both literature and cinema. What Fleming established, other authors have continued. Bond has been played by many actors, including Sean Connery, George Lazenby, Roger Moore, Timothy Dalton, Pierce Brosnan, and Daniel Craig, in more than twenty-five films. In 2018, there were rumors that the next Bond could be Idris Elba.

BOND COCKTAIL

2 ounces vodka
1 ounce champagne
½ ounce Pernod
1 sugar cube
Lemon twist

*Place the vodka in the freezer for at least one hour before
you plan to create this cocktail. Also place the cocktail glass
in the freezer. Soak the sugar in the Pernod at the bottom
of the frozen glass. Add the champagne and then the vodka.
Garnish with a lemon twist and serve.*

The fatal woman, seductive and mysterious—a proper spy
novel is incomplete without one. This book would also be incomplete without this Femme Fatale. Enjoy!

FEMME FATALE

2 ounces vodka
1 ounce crème de framboise
½ ounce lemon juice
½ ounce orange juice
¼ ounce honey water (equal parts honey and water)
10 raspberries

*Add ice and water to a cocktail glass to chill the glass. Add
ice to the tin side of a Boston shaker. In the mixing glass,
add the vodka, crème de framboise, lemon juice, orange*

juice, honey water, and raspberries. Pour the contents of the mixing glass into the iced tin and secure the glass to the tin. Shake the contents until the ice sounds different and the contents are cold. Empty the glass. Open the Boston shaker. Strain the contents of the shaker into the chilled glass. Serve.

A gun is the most identified weapon of a spy, but the dagger has several benefits in close quarters, such as maximum damage with little sound that might alert someone, exposing the spy. Small but handy, the dagger can also be used as a tool to access files or rooms.

DAGGER

½ ounce tequila
½ ounce crème de cacao
½ ounce peach schnapps

Prepare a shot glass. Add ice to the tin side of a Boston shaker. In the mixing glass, add the tequila, crème de cacao, and peach schnapps. Pour the contents of the mixing glass into the iced tin and secure the glass to the tin. Shake the contents until the ice sounds different and the contents are cold. Open the Boston shaker. Strain the contents into the shot glass. Serve.

Halle Berry is an all-American beauty and an Academy Award–winning actress. Berry is the whole package: beauty and substance. In 2002, Berry played NSA agent Giacinta "Jinx" Johnson opposite Pierce Brosnan as 007 in Lee Tamahori's *Die Another Day*.

AMERICAN BEAUTY SPECIAL

1 ounce triple sec
1 ounce cognac
1 ounce rum

Add ice and water to a cocktail glass to chill the glass. Add ice to the tin side of a Boston shaker. In the mixing glass, add the triple sec, cognac, and rum. Pour the contents of the mixing glass into the iced tin and secure the glass to the tin. Shake the contents until the ice sounds different and the contents are cold. Open the Boston shaker. Strain the contents of the shaker into the iced glass. Serve.

In the United States, the Fourth of July has a special meaning: freedom! I recommend this cocktail only for someone who is experienced behind the bar because whoever prepares the drink will have to flame the alcohol.

FOURTH OF JULY

⅔ ounce bourbon
⅔ ounce Galliano
⅔ ounce coffee liqueur
⅔ ounce orange juice
⅔ ounce heavy cream
Ground cinnamon

Warm a cocktail glass by pouring hot water into the cocktail glass and allowing it to sit for a minute. Discard the water. Add the bourbon and Galliano into the glass. With a match or lighter, flame the drink. Sprinkle the ground cinnamon on top of the flaming drink. Add ice to the tin side of a Boston shaker. In the mixing glass, add the coffee liqueur, orange juice, and heavy cream. Pour the contents of the mixing glass into the iced tin and secure the glass to the tin. Shake the contents until the ice sounds different and the contents are cold. Open the Boston shaker. Strain the contents of the shaker into the glass with bourbon and Galliano. Serve.

BIBLIOGRAPHY

Amis, Kingsley. *Everyday Drinking*. New York: Bloomsbury, 2008.

Arthur, Stanley Clisby. *Famous New Orleans Drinks and How to Mix 'Em*. Gretna, LA: Pelican, 1937. Reprints, 1944, 1965, 1972, 2013.

Bullock, Tom. *The Ideal Bartender*. St. Louis: Buxton & Skinner Printing and Stationary, 1917.

Burke, Harman Burney. *Burke's Complete Cocktail & Drinking Recipes: With Recipes for Food Bits for the Cocktail Hour*. New York: Books, 1936.

Crockett, Albert Stevens. *The Old Waldorf-Astoria Bar Book*. New York: A. S. Crockett, 1935.

Daly, Tim. *Daly's Bartenders' Encyclopedia*. Worchester, MA: Tim Daly, 1903.

Dick, Erma Biesel. *The Old House: Holiday & Party Cookbook*. New York: Cowles, 1969.

Duecy, Erica. *Storied Sips: Evocative Cocktails for Everyday Escapes, with 40 Recipes*. New York: Random House Reference, 2013.

Embury, David. *The Fine Art of Mixing Drinks: The Classic Guide to the Cocktail*. New York: Mud Puddle Books, 2008.

Federle, Tim. *Tequila Mockingbird: Cocktails with a Literary Twist*. Philadelphia: Running Press, 2013.

Haigh, Ted. *Vintage Spirits and Forgotten Cocktails: From the Alamagoozlum to the Zombie and Beyond*. Beverly, MA: Quarry Books, 2009.

Hearn, Lafcadio. *La Cuisine Creole: A Collection of Culinary Recipes from Leading Chefs and Noted Creole Housewives, Who Have Made New Orleans Famous for its Cuisine*. New Orleans: Hansell & Brothers, 1885.

Hess, Robert. *The Essential Bartender's Pocket Guide: Truly Great Cocktail Recipes*. New York: Mud Puddle Books, 2009.

Jackson, Michael. *Michael Jackson's Bar & Cocktail Companion: The Connoisseur's Handbook*. Philadelphia: Running Press, 1994.

Johnson, Harry. *Harry Johnson's 1882 New and Improved Bartender's Manual and a Guide for Hotels and Restaurants*. Newark, NJ: Charles E. Graham, 1882. Reprints, 1934, 2008.

Kappeler, George J. *Modern American Drinks: How to Mix and Serve All Kinds of Cups and Drinks*. New York: Merriam, 1895. Reprint, 2008.

Kosmas, Jason, and Dushan Zaric. *Speakeasy: Classic Cocktails Reimagined from New York's Employees Only Bar*. Berkeley, CA: Ten Speed, 2010.

Lipinski, Bob, and Kathie Lipinski. *The Complete Beverage Dictionary, 2nd edition*. New York: Van Nostrand Reinhold, 1996.

Meehan, Jim. *The PDT Cocktail Book: The Complete Bartender's Guide from the Celebrated Speakeasy*. New York: Sterling Epicure, 2011.

Miller, Dalyn, and Larry Donavan. *The Daily Cocktail: 365 Intoxicating Drinks and the Outrageous Events that Inspired Them*. Gloucester, MA: Fair Winds, 2006.

New York Bartenders' Association. *Official Handbook and Guide*. New York: New York Bartenders' Association, 1895.

Reed, Ben. *Ben Reed's Bartender's Guide*. New York: Ryland, Peters & Small, 2006.

Reekie, Jennie. *The London Ritz Book of Drinks: From Fine Wines and Fruit Punches to Cocktails and Canapes*. London: Ebury, 1990.

Rosenbaum, Stephanie. *The Art of Vintage Cocktails*. New York: Egg & Dart, 2013.

Schmid, Albert W. A. *The Kentucky Bourbon Cookbook*. Lexington, KY: University Press of Kentucky, 2010.

———. *The Manhattan Cocktail: A Modern Guide to the Whiskey Classic*. Lexington, KY: University Press of Kentucky, 2015.

———. *The Old Fashioned: An Essential Guide to the Original Whiskey Cocktail*. Lexington, KY: University Press of Kentucky, 2013.

———. *How to Drink Like a Mobster: Prohibition-Style Cocktails*. Bloomington, IN: Red Lighting Books, 2018.

Stanforth, Deirdre. *The New Orleans Restaurant Cookbook: The Colorful History and Fabulous Cuisine of the Great Restaurants of New Orleans*. Garden City, NY: Doubleday, 1967.

Thomas, Jerry. *Bar-tenders Guide: Containing Receipts for Mixing*. New York: Dick & Fitzgerald, 1887. Reprint, 2008.

Trader Vic. *Trader Vic's Bartender's Guide, Revised*. Garden City, NY: Doubleday, 1947. Reprint, 1972.

Wellmann, Molly. *Handcrafted Cocktails: The Mixologist's Guide to Classic Drinks for Morning, Noon & Night.* Cincinnati: Betterway Home, 2013.

Wondrich, David. *Imbibe!* New York: Perigee, 2007.

ALBERT W. A. SCHMID is a Gourmand Award winner and author of several books, including *The Old Fashioned: An Essential Guide to the Original Whiskey Cocktail*, *The Manhattan Cocktail: A Modern Guide to the Whiskey Classic*, *How to Drink Like a Mobster*, and *The Hot Brown: Louisville's Legendary Open-Faced Sandwich*.

Lightning Source UK Ltd.
Milton Keynes UK
UKHW050945240819
348488UK00006B/29/P